WORLD CUP WARRIORS

WORLD CUP WARRIORS

THE BOYS IN BLUE

VIJAY LOKAPALLY

ILLUSTRATIONS BY
AUSTIN COUTINHO

B L O O M S B U R Y

NEW DELHI • LONDON • OXFORD • NEW YORK • SYDNEY

BLOOMSBURY INDIA
Bloomsbury Publishing India Pvt. Ltd
Second Floor, LSC Building No. 4, DDA Complex, Pocket C – 6 & 7,
Vasant Kunj, New Delhi 110070

BLOOMSBURY, BLOOMSBURY INDIA and the Diana logo are
trademarks of Bloomsbury Publishing Plc

First published 2019

ISBN: 978-93-89165-23-4; eBook: 978-93-89165-40-1

2 4 6 8 10 9 7 5 3 1

Printed and bound in India by Replika Press Pvt Ltd

For
Akshay Lokapally

Contents

Author's Note

The 1983 World Cup winning team was the reason for limited overs cricket taking wings in India. The first two editions of the tournament in 1975 and 1979 saw India suffer humiliation, losing even to Sri Lanka, and winning just one of the six matches against East Africa. It may have won inspiring Test series overseas in West Indies and England in 1971, but India was considered a team least suited for shorter format of the game. All that changed in 1983 when Kapil Dev and his men turned the world upside down and created a new order in world cricket. An underdog had emerged as the champion and new heroes had come to capture the attention of the cricket fans.

The triumph of 1983 is well-documented. History was made at Lord's when West Indies, champions in 1975 and 1979, surrendered to India in one of the greatest upsets of sporting history. The West Indies has not entered a final in subsequent tournaments even though it has won the Champions Trophy in 2004 and the 2016 ICC World T20 tournament. For India, it was the beginning of a journey that saw the team regain the World Cup at home ground in 2011 after having won the inaugural ICC World T20 tournament.

Cricket has grown enormously over the world as a game wanting to acquire a universal look. It may lag behind football, tennis and athletics in global appeal but there are signs of cricket spreading to nations in Asia and Europe. With women's cricket too looking up and attracting spectators and sponsors with each passing season, the game is looking more competitive. The emergence of Afghanistan and Nepal is an encouraging sign of cricket administrators over the world.

The forthcoming World Cup in England is expected to be the biggest ever in terms of prize money and audience support. Most cricketers look forward to playing in England, which offers arguably the best of facilities. The cricket venues are top class, travelling time for the teams is quite comfortable and the format this time is the best since it allows each team an opportunity to overcome early setbacks, if any.

Most teams are well prepared, given the international calendar. The Indian Premier League (IPL) was an indication of the form and fitness of the many players, who have geared up for the event that showcases the best of world cricket. The

World Cup returns to England after 1999 when Australia won the last two encounters in stunning style, both against South Africa. The league victory, by two wickets in the final over, gave Australia the advantage after the semi-final between the teams ended in a tie.

The tournament will see many players make their World Cup debut and some take a bow at the end of it. Greats like Mahendra Singh Dhoni and Chris Gayle could well be making their final appearance in a World Cup. Dhoni, playing his fourth World Cup, obviously backs himself to sign off on a high after having led India to the crown in 2011. For Gayle, winning the World Cup has remained an unfulfilled dream after four attempts. He symbolises the essence of stroke-making even as the modern era is enriched with some entertainers like Virat Kohli, Rohit Sharma, Andre Russell, AB de Villiers (now retired), David Warner and Glenn Maxwell.

The 2019 edition is expected to produce high-scoring matches since cricket promoters in England prefer pitches that favour batsmen. The demands of the audience and the sponsors are uppermost in the minds of the organisers. Last-over finishes were the reason for the success of the 2019 IPL, and the World Cup in England would like to follow the same pattern. The weather conditions do offer challenges, since the ball may swing in some venues, but the organisers expect high-scoring encounters.

India is the favourite for many reasons. The team has a formidable batting line-up with Kohli, Shikhar Dhawan, Rohit Sharma, MS Dhoni and Kedar Jadhav promising to give their bowlers the cushion of a decent total to defend. The team boasts of the most versatile bowling attack where Jasprit Bumrah and Mohammed Shami have emerged as the best opening pair in the world with Bhuvaneshwar Kumar as a strong backup. In spinner Kuldeep Yadav, the team has a mystery element, while Hardik Pandya lends depth to the team's batting and bowling.

Australia is an eternal favourite. With the return of David Warner and Steve Smith, having completed their one-year ban following the ball-tampering episode, Australia can back themselves on the strength of being a well-balanced side. Usman Khawaja brings a calming influence on the batting line-up, which has the explosive Aaron Finch at the top and Shaun Marsh and Maxwell in the middle. Bowling could be a worry for Australia.

England has played some good cricket in the run-up to the World Cup and should consider themselves a strong contender. The team is led by Eoin Morgan, who can look for support from Jason Roy, Joe Root, Jos Buttler, Ben Stokes and Jonny Bairstow. Batting will be England's strength as the host will attempt to win their first ever World Cup.

Everyone loves the West Indies to excel on the world stage. The great combinations of 1975, 1979 and 1983 set high benchmarks in limited overs cricket but failed to system them. The team, after playing the semi-finals in 1996, never made the grade but experts are expecting a resurgence of West Indies cricket in England. Pakistan, for all their unpredictable nature, cannot be taken lightly and remains a contender. South Africa has been the most disappointing team in World Cup history, never living up their potential. A great at the league stage, they have come as a cropper in knockout situations.

For New Zealand, Sri Lanka, Afghanistan and Bangladesh, a place in the semi-final look like a dream against better-equipped opponents. Even given the uncertain factors of the game, it would be nothing short of a miracle for one of them to figure in the knockout stage.

The team with an incisive bowling attack is best placed to win the Cup. India and England lead the overall charge at the World Cup, which culminates at the iconic Lord's on July 14.

Foreword

I was two years old when India won its first cricket World Cup in 1983 at Lord's by beating the two-time champions, West Indies. That epic victory changed the face of Indian cricket. In my playing days, the conversations were dominated by the heroics of our World Cup-winning captain, my home-town hero—Kapil Dev. He was a great source of inspiration to my generation. My goal, like any other aspiring cricketer, was to represent India and win a World Cup. In 2000, I did get the taste of a World Cup win (in under-19). Later, I became the 134th One Day International (ODI) player to play for India.

I was a newcomer adjusting to international cricket. Having performed decently, I was picked for the 2003

Cricket World Cup, the first to be played in Africa. We did not have a great start, but the players started improving their performances as the tournament progressed. It was a fantastic learning process for me—playing against some formidable opponents in demanding conditions and pressure. I was also fortunate to be competing along with greats like Sachin Tendulkar, Rahul Dravid, Sourav Ganguly and Anil Kumble. The dressing room was a fantastic place to pick priceless lessons in cricket.

We excelled in the league, losing only to Australia, and taming Pakistan was a thrilling experience, with Tendulkar producing a scintillating 98. It remains one of my favourite Tendulkar innings. I can also never forget the sensational spell by Ashish Nehra against England at Durban when he claimed six wickets. Our journey took us to the final where Australia did nothing wrong. Ricky Ponting's attacking century took the game away from us, but I returned enriched with experience from my first ever World Cup.

The 2007 edition of the World Cup, in the West Indies, was heartbreaking. We exited in the first round itself. It was a lesson. We spent the next four years preparing for the World Cup to be played at home. There were such hype and excitement. We all wanted to win it for Sachin. It was known that it was going to be his final World Cup and I am so glad we could do it for him and the millions of fans of Indian cricket all over the world.

On the personal front, I was going through a difficult phase of life. During the tournament, I learnt of my dreadful medical condition, but nothing was going to stop me. I could do it only because of the support of my mother, Shabnam Singh, and my well-wishers. The World Cup had to be won. We had the best of playing conditions and a cracking outfit which shone under the captaincy of Mahi (MS Dhoni). It was a dream run and I still relive some of those glorious moments as we emulated the heroes of 1983. The best thing that came out of the win, personally, was YouWeCan—the foundation that I established to fight cancer and spread awareness about the disease.

I was privileged to be part of the 2007 ICC T20 World Cup triumph. It transformed the face of cricket. The shortest format of the game created the exciting Indian Premier League (IPL), which has helped so many players gain international recognition. The 2011 World Cup triumph was a dream come true as we won the Cup at the Wankhede Stadium and I bagged the Player of the Series award. Sachin was carried on the shoulders of various team members. As Virat (Kohli) rightly remarked, 'Sachin carried the burden of the nation for 21 years, so it is time we carried him on our shoulders.' That was a very touching tribute to the greatest cricketer the game has ever seen.

It is World Cup time again and we have a bunch of 15 stars all set to conquer the cricket world. I am glad the Cup is being held in England, which is such a convenient and attractive place to play and watch cricket. I must say, the Indian team is well prepared and looks favourite to win the Cup under Virat's captaincy. The presence of Mahi brings precious experience to the campaign and I have faith in the team to travel the distance.

The format of the Cup, where each team gets to play all other competitors, is an ideal concept that was first seen in 1992 when Australia and New Zealand had co-hosted the tournament. I am sure Virat Kohli's team is high on confidence. It has the best possible bowling attack in the tournament and the batting has tremendous depth too. It is going to be a highly competitive tournament, where no team will have a chance to relax.

I congratulate Bloomsbury India on publishing this book, *World Cup Warriors: The Boys in Blue*, with a profile of each member and an accompanying comment on them from a former World Cup player. I am glad that Vijay Lokapally has taken the time off from his hectic schedule to write on the current crop of World Cup aspirants.

Vijay *bhai*, as he is fondly called by my generation of cricketers, has seen the game from close quarters for more than three decades. He has written about me since my under-15 days. I have known him personally very well and benefited from his elderly advice on many occasions, not to forget his insightful reporting on the game. He commands respect in Indian cricket for his honest writing and integrity. What I have loved the most is how he would report on our domestic matches with the same dedication that marked his work on overseas assignments. I am sure the readers will appreciate his encouraging words on the World Cup-bound Indian warriors.

My best wishes to the Indian team and Vijay *bhai's* effort.

Mumbai **Yuvraj Singh**

MRF

Virat Kohli

CAPTAIN	
AGE	30 YEARS
PLAYING ROLE	TOP-ORDER BATSMAN
BATTING	RIGHT-HAND BAT
BOWLING	RIGHT-ARM MEDIUM
ODI MATCHES	227

Virat Kohli—a name in the hearts of cricket lovers, cricket enthusiasts, young and veterans, from the cricketing fraternity—is loved by all, critiqued by a few and envied by some for sure! He is known to deliver with his bat, in irrepressible style, and use his aggression to drive himself and his team to glory.

He challenges his opponents less and himself more. He performs with a conviction that inadvertently puts his opponents to the test. He treats every game with equal importance, and his rivals sense that in his fervour and demeanour. He is known to be a beast on the field—one who performs not only with his physical prowess but also with his mind. He is someone who has carved himself through practice, triumphs and defeats, and propels his attitude to its maximum potential.

Speaking of his batting style, he is not cumbersome in his approach and playmaking. Using a straightforward approach, he drives through the chase and offers a grand spectacle to the ones having their eyes glued on him. His batting has an aura of dominance that stems from his self-confidence. The unhurried tackling of the ball in the middle is a sight that delights the purists and the common man. It allows them to derive a certain amount of joy, which a few cricketers in world cricket can guarantee.

Virat is all about commitment—to the game and also to himself. He displays his passion through long-standing dedication and with pride. To be able to handle the pressure and yet deliver is a trait that certainly puts him in the category of the greats. He has the temperament of Sunil Gavaskar and the innovative skills of Viv Richards.

In contemporary cricket, he is the prized wicket that every bowler desires.

He is often in the news for the temper he exhibits on field. But the world has accepted his show. In fact, we all enjoy those moments when he replies to his opponent with an onslaught of runs. More so, when he indulges in an exchange of heated words. It does make it more exciting for the viewers with the realisation that it is all genuine and done in the spirit of the game. He is surely more appealing to the younger crowd since it clearly adds a distinct flavour to the personality of their favourite cricketer, batsman or even an idol that they revere. He is a brand on his own accord now—one who exudes confidence, a marketable personality, and of course, his flair for the game.

Virat serves as a hero for many not just because of his display at the crease but also for his character. He is the brand ambassador for a plethora of brands and companies. But he picks his deals based on his principles. He is known to have let go of some profitable contracts because he perceived them to be out of his character. This serves as a strong example to a generation that is exposed to all sorts of choices and prefers to adopt a faster approach to its goals. With many famous personalities endorsing brands and opinions which may not exactly serve as beneficial to the younger lot, Virat set himself as an example of one of a kind.

He is also respected as an icon at a time when there are only a handful of sports personalities that the younger generation idolises in a country which is the second most populated in the world, and thus expected to produce more champions. This does not mean that we are diminishing the achievements of other players in our country, but he serves as an example to the youth that a sportsperson can be hard-working, high achiever and, at the same time, makes a style statement of his own, which is sustained by a strong character. His achievements are further commendable owing to the fact that cricket is a highly competitive sport, especially in a cricket-frenzy country like India.

Virat is seen as a strong-willed sportsperson, who achieves whatever he has set his eyes on. He creates a vision for himself into which he also pulls in his fellow teammates. Leading the statistics for scoring the maximum number of runs while serving as the captain in One Day Internationals (ODIs), he is definitely the favourite to lift the World Cup, especially amongst the cricket fan base of India. With MS Dhoni by his side, he has ideal support and guidance to power through the championship. Dhoni's strategies and fielding tactics have always been remarkable and have drawn praises from the experts of the game. They can come in handy for Virat in times of need.

Pakistan is seen as the arch-rival, which has always been the case, in sports and otherwise. Pakistan boasts of a strong squad, which is prepared to take on the toughest of competition, including that from its closest adversary—India. It will be a spectacle to watch when India will meet Pakistan in the league stage of the tournament. Given the strained relationship between the two neighbouring countries, one can understand the enormous pressure that Virat and his team will likely to feel.

The match against Pakistan will no doubt be a test of mettle for Virat. History has witnessed that India has never lost a match to Pakistan in the World Cup in six meetings. The last win at Adelaide, in 2015, was built on the strength of a century by Virat. It was a tremendous start to India's campaign, which ended in a defeat in the semi-final to the eventual winner—Australia. But Virat left his mark on the tournament with a brilliant show combining his batting skills and captaincy strategies to win millions of hearts.

The exacting standards that Virat has set for himself will decide the course of the team at the World Cup. He is a shining example for the team, which believes it is best prepared for the tournament. Virat, thanks to his excellent rapport with coach Ravi Shastri and the national selection committee, has the team to go the distance. His strength as a batsman holds the key to India's effort to reclaim the Cup. He has, needless to say, the best wishes of the nation.

Kapil Dev on Virat Kohli

The best man to lead India on such a daunting mission. I have, like millions of cricket lovers, followed him from the time he had arrived at the international stage. His rise has been rapid and huge. I must say, he has matured amazingly from the time he has taken over the captaincy from Dhoni. I know he has been criticised for being aggressive, sometimes brash, but that was how he played his game. He may have looked childish to some but there was never any doubt that he was challenging himself to take his game to the next level. He was instinctive four years ago, but he has mellowed. You can see the difference in how he seeks reviews from the third umpire. He does not mind consulting his colleagues, and that is a sign of maturity. His understanding of the game has improved and he is a much better captain now. He has become a leader. His batting and captaincy will be crucial. Of course, he will need the team to respond to his demands and deliver too. And he has already got a great one.

Kapil Dev, one of the greatest cricketers, was the captain of the team, which won the 1983 World Cup. In all, he played four World Cups—1979, 1983, 1987 and 1992.

Rohit Sharma

VICE-CAPTAIN	
AGE	31 YEARS
PLAYING ROLE	TOP-ORDER BATSMAN
BATTING	RIGHT-HAND BAT
BOWLING	RIGHT-ARM OFFBREAK
ODI MATCHES	206

Sunil Gavaskar is not an easy person to please. A player has to be very good to extract the praise—'he is good'— from the master. But Rohit Sharma ranks high in Gavaskar's list. He may not be Rohit's greatest admirer but when the master says 'Rohit can become the most destructive batsman after Viv Richards and Virender Sehwag', the cricket world takes note. In a newspaper column, Gavaskar once acknowledged that Rohit was a special batsman. Had his coach, Dinesh

Lad, not discovered Rohit's batting skills by accident, the Mumbai cricketer may have ended up as a bowler.

It so happened that Lad's team was playing a local final where Rohit's team was bundled out at 67. 'The target was a walkover literally, but he bowled two overs that stood out. I saw a match-winning bowler in him,' recalled Lad. Rohit, having come under Lad's scrutiny, was asked to join his coaching academy. Thus began an association that changed the youngster's life forever.

Rohit's journey is almost like folklore. His parents lived in Dombivli, a suburb of Mumbai, where he did not have access to good cricket facilities. They were reserved for the city boys. 'I have seen many players from the suburbs leave the game because they did not get level playing field. Without adequate coaching and training facilities, it was hard for them to compete with the city boys,' said Lad, who lost little time in shifting Rohit from Dombivli to Borivali to enable him to enjoy proper cricket coaching.

Coming closer to the city was no assurance for Rohit to pursue cricket. He had to attend school, which meant coughing up a monthly fee. It was a challenge. Rohit, the first grandchild in the family, was brought up at his uncle's place. The Telugu-speaking parents of Rohit willingly allowed the move to facilitate their son's love for cricket at the Swami Vivekanand School, where Lad was the coach.

'His uncle needed to be persuaded to send Rohit to this school. He was very reluctant, and it took me time to discover his predicament,' remembered Lad. It was tough for Rohit's uncle to pay the monthly school fee of Rs 275. The donation had been waived but the monthly fee had to be paid. Lad was imparting cricket coaching for free at the school and requested the authorities to make an exception in Rohit's case. 'He was very good at cricket and I pleaded with the principal to waive off the monthly tuition fees. I was so relieved when the principal agreed,' said Lad. It was the turning point in Rohit's career.

Rohit made news in Mumbai cricket with his brilliant performances, not as a bowler, as Lad had initially visualised, but as a batsman. Lad noted:

> One day I was late for the coaching and saw a batsman at a distance, with his back towards me, knocking the ball. He played the ball exceptionally well. I observed him for an over or so and when I went closer, I discovered it was Rohit. His batting was brilliant. That day I discovered Rohit, the batsman. Can you imagine that he was reluctant to share his love for batting only because I had asked him to concentrate on his off-spin?

He made 140 in his first match, as an opener, for his school team.

Once Rohit had access to coaching facilities, his cricket career took off as he made waves in the Harris Shield (under-16) as an under-14 kid. His rise was rapid and Mumbai's cricket circuit took note of the stroke player who batted beyond his age. Former Indian batsman Pravin Amre noted:

> To me, he was a typical product of Mumbai cricket. Learning the game in the maidans made him highly competitive, and his talent ensured that his progress remained steady. He made an early impact and I am glad he has risen to become one of the trusted batsmen for the team.

Rohit has gained a lot from his preparations before every tour. Playing the rising ball hurled from a distance of 16 yards on cement pitches brushed up his shots square of the wicket. The pull and cut, not to forget the cover-drive, became his profitable shots. Observers believed that Rohit had more time than any batsman in Indian cricket to play the ball. It was his temperament that let him down when he lost his place in the team for the 2011 World Cup.

International debut in 2007 was a deserving recognition for Rohit. He was a part of the team that won the inaugural ICC T20, and he remained a constant member for the next two seasons. The launching of the Indian Premier League (IPL) impacted his cricket. Diversions from the game meant he had lost his focus. 'I spoke to him, scolded him and reminded him that he must give time to his cricket,' said Lad. To Rohit's credit, the student obeyed his teacher and dedicated himself to the game he loved so much.

Ten years after his T20 debut, Rohit arrived on the Test scene with a bang by hitting back-to-back centuries. His 177 in his debut and 111 not out in Sachin Tendulkar's farewell Test were memorable innings. Rohit had come into the Test following a sensational 209 against Australia in an One Day International (ODI) at Bangalore. He was to hit two more ODI double hundreds—264 against Australia at Kolkata in 2014 and 208 not out against Sri Lanka at Mohali in 2017.

Lazy elegance marks his batting. 'Right-handed David Gower'—as observed by a cricketer once. Gower was known for his silken stroke play and sweet timing, which also adorns Rohit's show at the crease. His best qualities include absorbing pressure and the skill to bat at any position. This flexibility to be ready to bat at any position has helped Rohit, who now carries a huge responsibility as an opener.

His partnership with Shikhar Dhawan holds the key for India's success in ODIs.

In the last World Cup, Rohit aggregated 330 runs in eight matches. He would aim to surpass that figure in 2019. In form, he promises to do that.

Manoj Prabhakar on Rohit Sharma

He carries the burden at the top. For all his talent and skills, Rohit would have to fall back on his experience of more than a decade in international cricket. The Mumbai school of cricket has nurtured him well because he has managed to cement his place in the team with some consistent scores. I am very impressed by the way he has backed himself. He has the example of David Warner, who hardly looked he had not played for more than a year. The team needs a batsman who does not get carried away because one-day cricket is not just about hitting every ball. I think his shot selection is judicious and he is able to force the pace by rotating the strike. It is his best quality. He is a match-winner and should be treated like one. He must watch the ball closely in England.

Manoj Prabhakar was one of the finest all-rounders and played in three editions of the World Cup in 1987, 1992 and 1996.

Shikhar Dhawan

AGE	33 YEARS
PLAYING ROLE	OPENING BATSMAN
BATTING	LEFT-HAND BAT
BOWLING	RIGHT-ARM OFFBREAK
ODI MATCHES	128

Not a single member of the Delhi (U-16) team, who played the Vijay Merchant Trophy match at Patiala in the winter of 1999, earned the India cap except a wiry 14-year-old named Shikhar Dhawan. At that point too he was a happy-go-lucky trainee from the Sonnet Club. His coach, Tarak Sinha, had high hopes from this boy and would organise a special session for the left-hander, who played with distinct style and flair. His timing of the ball was exceptional and Dhawan could pack a punch too in his square drive. 'There was something about the boy and I could sense he was destined to go far. Only he had to keep his head on the shoulders,' was how Sinha remembered his student.

Sinha was right. Ten years from the time he appeared for Delhi in that junior grade match, Dhawan made his One Day International (ODI) debut against Australia in a home series. He travelled to the West Indies, made just 69 runs in four ODIs, and lost his place. That was the darkest phase of his life. Unable to find a way back to the national team, he slowly lost his focus and reached a stage where he was contemplating moving away from cricket. Frustration gripped him and left Sinha worried. The coach counselled his pupil and Dhawan gave himself one more chance. Bowlers suffered at the hands of his bat in domestic cricket and Dhawan was back in the reckoning for the Test series against Australia at home. He was not going to let go of this hard-earned opportunity.

It was a debut scripted by the cricket gods. Dhawan tore apart the Australian attack with some incredible shotmaking. There were silken drives and robust cuts as Dhawan got into the history books with a century in his Test debut, emulating the great GR Viswanath. So impressed was

Viswanath by Dhawan's classical batting that he wanted to get in touch with the youngster to congratulate him. When Dhawan heard this, he lost little time in contacting the maestro. 'Such a humble boy,' remarked Viswanath, and also exclaimed, 'What a knock I say!' It indeed was a sterling demonstration of attacking batting by Dhawan, who sadly missed the next Test on account of a finger injury. But he had assured himself a place in the team. Sinha was relieved. So was Dhawan's batting coach Madan Sharma, who had worked tirelessly in trying to motivate his favourite pupil.

Having established himself in the team, Dhawan gave himself the freedom to sometimes experiment with his style—although not always with success. His learning process continued and he improved with every season. His slot at the top was assured when he returned to the ODI team for the 2013 Champions Trophy in England. His first two visits to the crease fetched him 114 against South Africa and 102 not out against the West Indies. Another half-century against Sri Lanka showed the tremendous form he was in. India went on to win the Champions Trophy with a win over England in the final, and Dhawan was crowned as the Man of the Series.

Dhawan figured in the Indian team for the 2015 ICC World Cup in Australia, where he managed to showcase his skills in three matches—73 against Pakistan, 137 against the West Indies and 100 against Ireland. He smashed a fiery 45 in the semi-final against Australia, but India's journey came to a disappointing end in its campaign to retain the World Cup. Eight centuries since that loss to Australia have shown Dhawan to be a reliable batsman at the top, in the company of Rohit Sharma. These two form, possibly, the most lethal opening pair in contemporary cricket.

Former stalwarts call Dhawan a value addition to the batting line-up. His temperament, not compromising with his natural flair to hit the ball, makes him the batsman to dread. His batting follows the top-gear pattern because he needs little time to settle. He often gets cracking from the first ball and he rubs his confidence in his partner, who is a significant part of India's campaign at the World Cup.

Bad shot or good shot is decided by the course the ball follows. Dhawan's view, expressed in an interview in *The Hindu*, is:

> The end result is the remuneration for your effort. Sometimes you have to play cross-batted and take smart risks. I always back my shots. I know this particular shot gives me runs. It can also cost me my wicket. I have to accept it because only I know what is best for me. It is

not that I am irresponsible because I get out playing shots.

Dhawan's dominance at the crease is a pleasant mix of aggression and caution and comes off as a confident man off the field. He can talk on religion for hours, loves horse riding, practices meditation, is involved in constant introspection of his game and spends time in analysing his opponents. 'It's not rocket science. Simple lessons I have learnt in life and on the cricket field,' he revealed his approach to the game.

In the cricket circuit, Dhawan is an enigma. He loves a confrontation on the field but buries the differences once the contest is over. Among his admirers is Ashish Nehra, who has referred to him as 'Shikhar *befiqar* (unperturbed)'. Dhawan never carries his cricket woes to home. His moustache and his slap on the thigh on taking a catch has made him popular amongst wrestlers. Dhawan welcomes them to his ever-growing fan club.

After three years of learning, Dhawan let out a secret in 2018. He said:

Hi guys. Wanted to share something that's very dear to my heart and is a different side to me. For the last three years, I've been learning to play the flute (my favourite instrument). I've had the privilege of taking lessons from Guru Venugopal Ji. I still have a long way to go but I'm glad I've started.

His batting is sweet music to his teammates, who now look forward to a calming session with his flute during the World Cup.

K Srikkanth on Shikhar Dhawan

Not because I was an opener, it is a crucial batting position in any format. The responsibility of giving a flying start is huge since it dictates the course of the contest, regardless of whether you are setting a target or chasing one. I think Shikhar is one of the finest openers in the game and I love the way he gets going without losing much time. He gives confidence to his partner by laying some daring shots, which can demoralise the best of bowlers. He has a natural instinct to attack and that is what he should stick to. True, the ball may seam and swing but the pitches are mostly going to be good for batting. I would like him to play out his strength. I say with experience that bowlers don't like it when they are attacked early and I expect Shikhar to do well.

K Srikkanth was an explosive opener who played the World Cup in 1983, 1987 and 1992.

Vijay Shankar

AGE	28 YEARS
PLAYING ROLE	ALLROUNDER
BATTING	LEFT-HAND BAT
BOWLING	RIGHT-ARM MEDIUM
ODI MATCHES	09

Three years ago, he stood at the entrance of the stadium in Nagpur and wondered what lay ahead. Close to the end of 2016, his cricket was obviously not progressing at the rate he had planned and the increasing competition around him made Vijay Shankar insecure and apprehensive. His ambitions were modest and realistic but he needed a break. His batting skills were well-documented and he had begun to work on his bowling too. 'I fancy myself as an all-rounder,' he had remarked then. That he backed himself and made an impression on the national selectors only shows Shankar's splendid work ethics and self-belief.

Securing a place in the World Cup team after only nine One Day Internationals (ODIs) to his credit has brought Shankar into international focus. In a team where Virat Kohli, Shikhar Dhawan, Rohit Sharma, MS Dhoni, Kedar Jadhav and Rohit Sharma have been saddled with the task of run-scoring, Shankar brings added value with his ability to bat with assurance and, if need be, take up the additional burden of bowling a few overs.

Former India opener WV Raman, who has monitored and mentored Shankar from his early days, was clear that in terms of progress, the Tamil Nadu cricketer had come a long way. Raman noted:

> I don't think he was aware of his own potential. He was initially short on confidence, which came because of the fact that he was in and out of the team. But there never was any doubt about his talent. With each season, he was becoming stronger and not selling short of himself.

To Shankar's credit, he did not allow the initial setbacks to impact his cricket. His approach to the game improved when he decided to project himself as a bowler. If there was any sense of insecurity, he managed to cross that phase. As Raman pointed out:

> His evolution has not been an overnight development. He may have been slow, but he has been steady—taking one step at a time. It will now depend on the situation he will be asked to handle and also a lucky break. At that level, you have to have some support from Lady Luck too.

Former players in Tamil Nadu learnt about Shankar through regular news in the local media. He was making waves in the Chennai League. For Raman, it was a 'pleasant' development. He reflected on Shankar's early days and said:

> When I returned to Tamil Nadu as a coach (after a stint in Bengal), I realised he was keen to play. Unfortunately, I was not able to fit him in the top order. I told him that he needed to work on his bowling so that I could find a place for him as a third seamer. Once (S) Badrinath moved out of Tamil Nadu, I managed to find a regular berth for Shankar.

The 2014–2015 Ranji Trophy season was a decisive phase for Shankar. His 95 against Mumbai in the league was a pleasant precursor to his performance in the knockout, where he was at his best. Shankar constructed his knocks around needs of the team, and his sequence of 111 and 82 (against Vidarbha), 91 (against Maharashtra) and 103 (against Karnataka) brought him to the national limelight. Shankar had finally broken his shackles.

Shankar had spent his initial time in the state team trying to be a regular. His plans to expand his base and work on his game had to be put on hold, even though Raman had immense faith in him. 'He did not believe when I said he should soon be playing for India. I told him not to be stifled by circumstances,' said Raman. With a guide like Raman by his side, Shankar's career took off and he was soon talked of as an India prospect.

His entry to the Indian team may have surprised a few but his place was never under any doubt. The selectors had zeroed on him for the fact that he was a multi-dimensional player. The Chairman of the selection committee MSK Prasad remarked while announcing the team that Shankar brought extra value to the process. 'He is a multi-dimensional player and can fill the role in the middle order,' Prasad had said.

As far as the team management is concerned, Shankar can perform the role of a floater. He can bat and bowl. He can field extraordinarily at any position. He can also bat at any position. He has the capacity to be a floater because he is technically a good batsman. Even though Shankar had been talked of as the possible no. 4 batsman, he can come in handy at any position from 1 to 6.

The fact that Shankar backs himself to play the role of a floater takes the pressure off him. If the conditions assist the seam bowlers, Shankar can hang in and take charge of the batting. He knows that thinking and executing do not go hand in hand. He has to accept things as they come and stop worrying about other aspects which are not under his control. He has learnt his lessons from the dismal show in the final of the Nidahas T20 Trophy against Bangladesh when he batted 19 balls to make 17 runs. Dinesh Karthik pulled off an exceptional win by hitting a six off the last ball. 'I would definitely say that the Nidahas Trophy was a life-changing experience as a cricketer for me,' he said in an interview to IANS (Indo-Asian News Service).

That innings taught him how to handle tough situations. He did not lose time in coming out of that setback that saw him being criticised. He did realise that he had to be more consistent to be able to justify his potential and there was no room to relax. Five ODI innings have not seen him cross the half-century yet. He can look forward to scoring big at the World Cup. The team needs Shankar to be at his best. He knows it too and is prepared to take on the mantle of a floater, the man to go to for Virat Kohli.

Yashpal Sharma on Vijay Shankar

When we played the World Cup, it was made clear that you would stick to the position allotted. If I was an opener, I would only replace an opener. Well, I did bat at nos 4, 5 and

6, but they were all in the middle order. I was given the no. 4 slot in the last three matches of the tournament.

No. 4 is a key position and I think Vijay is well suited to handle it. India's middle order is not the best in the World Cup. I would be happy to be proved wrong. Vijay has been picked because the selectors felt his temperament would carry him past strong opponents. I am sure he will take the responsibility of the middle order and must remember that the other teams would have done their homework on India. Vijay has the skills and the game to emerge as a match-winner. Remember, he can bowl too.

Yashpal Sharma was a star batsman of the 1983 World Cup, excelling in the opening match against the West Indies.

MS Dhoni

AGE	37 YEARS
PLAYING ROLE	WICKETKEEPER BATSMAN
BATTING	RIGHT-HAND BAT
BOWLING	RIGHT-ARM MEDIUM
ODI MATCHES	342

Hailing from Ranchi, a small town in Bihar (now the capital of Jharkhand), Mahendra Singh Dhoni beat all odds to reach the zenith that he is at today. The journey was not an easy one for him. Initially, he excelled at badminton and then at football. It was only his football coach at school, Keshav Banerjee, who sensed and recognised the cricket gene in him. After showing impressive wicketkeeping skills, Dhoni kicked off his journey for a successful and stellar cricketing career.

He comes from a region which does not feature cricket considerably as some other regions of the country. Bihar, where Dhoni remembers his early cricketing days, is a part of East India. It was West, North and South India that have been to be the powerhouses of cricket, providing the platform to many famous cricketers who made it big at the international level.

With minimal support, Dhoni crafted his own future. He surely received guidance and push from coaches and key people from cricket associations, but that only happened when his raw talent was being recognised from time to time. His success is to be attributed to his hard work and dedication.

It was necessarily his talent that paved his way to the Indian team. His batting skills and powerful shots shone through in his formative years when he performed to promote the Central Coal Fields Limited team to the 'A' division of junior cricket in Bihar. This period of cricketing success was instrumental for Dhoni in making it to the junior state team. The journey had begun.

Though initially unsuccessful at getting selected for the East Zone U-19 squad, since Bihar had finished only fourth in a tournament of six teams, in 1998, it was only in the next season (1999–2000) when his batting exploits in the Cooch Behar Trophy earned him a spot in the East Zone U-19 team. They lost the final against Punjab, which was served well by a youngster called Yuvraj Singh—Dhoni's future teammate in the Indian team. Yuvraj slammed 358 and provided early indications of his awesome prowess with the bat. But Dhoni's talent was not opaque and he went on to push his credentials in the domestic circuit.

He made his Ranji Trophy debut for Bihar in 1999–2000 at a young age of 18. From there onwards, his way to the Indian team seemed certain. His bold and hard-hitting batting style was seen at many stages in the coming years. From being discovered at talent-spotting initiatives in Jharkhand, reports of his performances were noted at the National Cricket Academy. Consistent success ensured a slot in the Indian 'A' team and Dhoni grew into a sensational phenomenon—someone who could not be missed in the crowd.

Seen as a strong character on and off the field, Dhoni's key trait is his style that is marked by courage and self-assurance. He is known to deliver in times of crisis. A key example would be the World Cup final of 2011 against Sri Lanka at Mumbai. When India lost Virender Sehwag and Sachin Tendulkar cheaply, Dhoni stepped on the crease by promoting himself in the order to script India's victory along with Gautam Gambhir, who provided superb support. Dhoni scored 91 to shape India's victory. The final would remain etched in the memories of cricket fans for years to come.

Dhoni has always been a fan favourite and an icon to uncountable youngsters from around the globe. His personality is underlined by his composure and self-control. There's certainly a reason why he is called 'Captain Cool'! He is strong, level-headed and brave when there is absolutely a need for someone to be so. He knows how to play the 'lone wolf'.

Known to carry the Indian team to victory on numerous occasions, Dhoni gained much favour to act as the captain of the Indian team. Recognised for his tactics and strategies, especially when it comes to setting fielding patterns and picking bowlers to unnerve the batsmen, he has emerged as the master plotter, easily one of the best captains in Indian cricket.

Staying away from controversies is Dhoni's hallmark. He is a highly respected player amongst his peers and professionals from the cricketing industry. Though the recent incident, where he walked into the field from the dugout to confront the umpire for his decision during the IPL (Indian Premier League) match against Rajasthan

Royals, was a first of its kind and certainly forgettable. It was not expected of Dhoni to resort to such behaviour. Captain Cool appeared so very human that day, arguing with the umpires at Jaipur. He got away lightly, but it was an image that certainly jolted his fans.

As Dhoni prepares for his fourth World Cup, he emerges as one of the greatest ambassadors for the game. Written off after the 2015 World Cup, Dhoni, with his dedication and supreme fitness, has kept his place in the team on merit. His athleticism is second to none and he is adept at beating the youngsters on the circuit hollow with his enthusiasm to compete. Dhoni has never compromised his commitment to the game, and his integrity is documented in glorious terms.

It is a fact that Dhoni is a captain's delight. As he stands behind the stumps, shouting encouraging words for the bowler, guiding the fielder a yard here or a yard there, Dhoni's involvement in the action stands out. There is not a moment when he stays quiet. A true sportsman, he led the team with distinction, when seniors like Sachin Tendulkar, Rahul Dravid, Sourav Ganguly and Virender Sehwag played under his captaincy. Later, wanting to extend his career by concentrating on the shorter formats of the game, he gave up the position to allow Virat Kohli to take over the responsibility in 2017.

At 38, Dhoni's image remains unaffected by that incident at Jaipur as he continues to be praised by one and all. Such episodes only add to the repertoire of loving recollections that we have of Dhoni. We will always admire him for his style of aggressive batting, some robust shots, for his cool style at the crease and mostly for the loving human being that he is.

Kiran More on MS Dhoni

Who can speak on Dhoni? None. Honestly, he is possibly the best known player in this tournament, who has entertained cricket lovers since his debut in 2004. He is the key to India's success in the biggest stage of one-day cricket. Can you imagine one moment of action without Dhoni in the frame when India is fielding? He is constantly in conversation with the bowlers, suggesting the field and on what line to bowl, guiding the team as a whole. His reading of the game and the judgement he makes in critical situations are exemplary. I don't think anyone can read the pitch better than him. He is the man to go to for Virat. His presence at the crease, when batting is the strength, can propel India to win the crown. His approach to batting is dictated by a calm mind. He is the best batsman to deal with death overs. Dhoni is my man for all seasons.

Kiran More was a reliable wicketkeeper at the World Cup in 1987 and 1992.

INDIA

Kedar Jadhav

AGE	34 YEARS
PLAYING ROLE	BATTING ALLROUNDER
BATTING	RIGHT-HAND BAT
BOWLING	RIGHT-ARM OFFBREAK
ODI MATCHES	59

Kedar Jadhav is a self-made cricketer. From tennis ball cricket, where he would jump from one match to another during the course of a day, he graduated to leather ball cricket with such ease that his coaches were convinced he was a natural. A product of local cricket from Pune, he dreamt big and made it to the Indian team from a city which prided in its cricket culture.

Starting from Prof. DB Deodhar, Chandu Borde, Hemant Kanitkar and his son Hrishikesh, Pune offered a stream of cricketers who did the state proud. Deodhar played first-class cricket with distinction and then served the game as an administrator and a selector. Borde was one of the finest batsmen, who bowled leg spin too, to dominate the game in the 1960s. The Kanitkars played Test cricket but ended up being underachievers. There were a few like Milind Gunjal, Shrikant Kalyani, Shantanu Sugwekar, Pandurang Salgaonkar and Surendra Bhave, who promised to make it big in the higher grade but lost out to better talent.

Jadhav, by making it to the World Cup team, adds to the cricket lustre of Maharashtra that has often complained of being given a step-motherly treatment by the national selectors. Jadhav too had to struggle at every level but his determination to play for India grew with every challenge he faced before he made his One Day International (ODI) debut in 2014. Not an all-rounder in the truest sense, he does provide with his off-spin.

Jadhav began his learning process at the Deccan Gymkhana and moved to the PYC Gymkhana after five years. It turned out to be a great move for Jadhav as he came in contact with Bhave, and his career took an upswing. Cricket was the sole purpose of Jadhav's life and he became a keen student of the game, even though he did not allow an overdose of coaching. Bhave wanted to preserve his natural instincts and it worked well for Jadhav.

Bhave saw him first during the 2003–2004 season. Bhave fondly remembered that time and said:

> I was attending a Ranji Trophy camp and there was this Cooch Behar (under-19) match at the Nehru Stadium where Maharashtra was playing against Kerala. I saw this youngster scoring runs at will and playing shots to all corners of the ground. There was something about his stroke play that convinced me that he was special. I found out that he was Kedar Jadhav, a promising middle-order batsman. His dominance was of a veteran batsman.

In that match, Jadhav slammed 195 as Maharashtra won the quarter-final with conviction.

Tennis ball cricket has a simple philosophy—see the ball and hit the ball. The batsman has to just hit his bat to the ball. Jadhav had learnt to master this style and was a much sought-after youngster on the Pune cricket circuit. He was to make the best of that experience in the 2012–2013 season when he scored a scintillating 327 against Uttar Pradesh in the Ranji Trophy match at Pune. Earlier, his best was in a practice game at the PYC where he made 220 in a match reduced to 43 overs a side due to rain.

The 2013–2014 season saw Jadhav arrive on the national scene in style as he aggregated over 1000 runs as Maharashtra made it to the Ranji Trophy final where it lost to Karnataka. The season included a match against Mumbai, where Jadhav came up with a sterling century in the second innings to convince the national selectors that he belonged to the big league.

Bhave recalled that knock—'It was possibly the best seaming attack I had seen. Shardul Thakur was making the ball talk and Zaheer Khan was darting the ball around. It was a nightmare to bat there and Kedar scored a century in that quarter-final.' Having conceded a first innings lead of 122 to Mumbai, the target was 252 as Maharashtra bowled the opposition out for 129 in the second innings. Jadhav scored an unbeaten 120 to stun Mumbai.

Jadhav's selection for the World Cup came amidst stiff competition. Ambati Rayudu was considered the favourite but Jadhav, with his ability to bowl off-spin, won the race. He adds value to the team's campaign because he is adept at soaking in the pressure. His technique allows him to play with freedom since he looks to attack at the first opportunity. His bowling reflects his temperament—fearless and competitive.

There is an interesting story that highlights his determination. The High Performance Committee of the Maharashtra Cricket Association (MCA) had decided on a camp of 20 players in Nasik. Jadhav's name did not figure in the list. On Bhave's request, the MCA agreed to add four more players to enable practice matches between two teams. Jadhav grabbed the chance by scoring heavily and forcing his way into the Ranji Trophy team. To this day, Jadhav remembers how it became a 24-member camp just to accommodate him. To his credit, he did not let his mentor down. He made a modest debut against Tamil Nadu, lost his place in the side before the season was over, but returned next year to cement his place.

Jadhav, a middle-order batsman with a wide range of strokes, is considered a match-winner. His temperament is his greatest asset and the team management realises his potential too. An unbeaten 105 against Zimbabwe in his fourth ODI was enough to boost his confidence and he gave ample display five innings later when he produced a sensational 120 against England at Pune. Faced with a daunting target of 351, India was thankful for Jadhav's

76-ball knock. To be awarded Man of the Match in front of his home crowd was a memorable feat for Jadhav.

'I am very happy for Kedar. He may have got into the Indian team late but deserved a place in the World Cup squad. His experience will be an asset to the team in English conditions,' said Bhave, who was the best player from Maharashtra but did not earn the India cap. He has lived that dream through his trusted pupil.

Kirti Azad on Kedar Jadhav

He is a gritty customer. Watching him, I go back to the time when we would look to chip in with the ball too apart from only contributing to the bat. I fancied myself as an all-rounder because I had the confidence to bowl. Kedar promises to deliver with the ball and one has seen him do that often. His action makes it difficult for the batsman to pick him, as he kind of slides the ball low and hard. His batting is sound. He does not abandon his natural game and goes about his business as confidently as any other member of the team. He can play a key role by coming good in the middle order and come in if a regular bowler does not perform his responsibility. I expect Kedar to emerge as a key player in this tournament with his sound batting and innovative stuff with the ball. He brings depth to the team.

Kirti Azad was a flamboyant batsman who also shone with the ball in the 1983 World Cup.

Dinesh Karthik

AGE	33 YEARS
PLAYING ROLE	WICKETKEEPER BATSMAN
BATTING	RIGHT-HAND BAT
BOWLING	-
ODI MATCHES	91

Most wicketkeepers, who took to cricket in the 1990s, drew inspiration from Syed Kirmani, who was a part of the 1983 World Cup winning team. His work behind the stumps was a key factor, especially the catch in the final to get rid of Faoud Bacchus, in plucking the catch in front of the first slip. It was right out of a fairy tale, as India forced an epic win and the world came to applaud the team's skills at one-day cricket.

Dinesh Karthik, who was barely two years old when India won the Cup at Lord's, was among those who watched Kirmani achieve the glory through videos. Kirmani was followed by Kiran More, Chandrakant Pandit, Nayan Mongia, Parthiv Patel, Ajay Ratra, Deep Dasgupta and Rahul Dravid, who also donned the gloves in One Day Internationals (ODIs). For Karthik, the elevation to the Indian team in 2004 was the result of his hard work.

He made his debut in an ODI against England at Lord's. In the low-scoring match, he pulled off a stumping and a catch as India won the contest. Two months later, Karthik played his first Test cricket at Mumbai against Australia. It was literally baptism of fire because the pitch was a minefield and keeping was a nightmare. But Karthik earned praise for his performance and grew in strength with every season.

Karthik, in the opinion of national selectors, was preferred to Rishabh Pant because of his experience. The debate involving Karthik and Pant was settled after giving both plenty of chances, but the choice fell on Karthik who had 91 ODIs to his credit. True, Pant had the backing of most former players, but Karthik won the race because the team management also gave its approval to this Tamil Nadu cricketer.

There can be no doubt that Karthik is ready for the World Cup. His appearance in the World Cup, if at all, would depend only on Dhoni if he cannot make it on account of an injury. 'I can't see Dhoni being dropped for poor form,' said former Test wicketkeeper Syed Kirmani. Having followed Dhoni's career closely, Kirmani, who was also a national selector, was only airing the views of a large section of cricket followers.

Karthik and Patel did not get many opportunities because of Dhoni's presence. Dhoni was indispensable since he was the first choice of every captain he played under. Now Karthik, at 33, can be called adequately matured to don the mantle of the wicketkeeper in case of an emergency.

He has won crucial matches for India in the past. His last-ball six to help India win the final of 2018 Nidahas Trophy against Bangladesh was sensational. He arrived at the crease with India needing 34 off 12 balls and it boiled down to five off the last delivery to be bowled by Soumya Sarkar. With a cool mind, Karthik picked the wide half volley to send it sailing over extra cover—a tough shot in a tough situation. 'Memory for a lifetime' was how he described his emotions.

Karthik was easily the best to qualify for the World cup team. His value to the team is understood well by the insiders. He is known to give priceless inputs to the captain and the bowlers. He is also adept at making the decision to ask for the DRS (Umpire Decision Review System). It is a judgement that can prove crucial as a DRS wasted can cost the team dearly. To guide the bowler or the captain to ask for a DRS is the job of the wicketkeeper and Karthik is considered to be reliable in this department.

In Indian cricket, Karthik is rated high as a finisher. A batsman has to have the right temperament and the range of shots to finish a game against heavy odds. He had always aspired for a batting slot higher in the order before offering his services as a possible finisher. What works in Karthik's favour is his ability to play seam and spin. He also helps the team by never overreacting in a difficult situation. Overall, he is a balanced package.

On his selection, Karthik said:

> I am very excited. It has been a dream for me to be a part of this team for a long time now. As a team, we have done some special things. I have been through that journey and I have really wanted to be a part of this team.

Jacques Kallis, the South African great cricketer, as the coach of Kolkata Knight Riders was happy for Karthik. In an interview to *Sportstar*, Kallis said:

> He is a very experienced player and knows his game pretty well. He has got us out of many [tricky] situations in the past. He has an all-round view of the game, which can also help the youngsters. It gives you an edge. He will certainly be in my team.

Karthik is an ideal wicketkeeper. In Kirmani's words:

> The job of a wicketkeeper is to be the guide to his captain and bowlers. He has to look for the weaknesses of the opponents and lift the morale of his teammates. Other than umpires, he is the one watching every ball closely. He also learns to read the pitch well. To me, a wicketkeeper is the no. 1 man in the team. I remember, in 1983, Kapil Dev was the captain of the team, but he said at the first team meeting that he had a lot to learn from his seniors. That galvanised us.

Karthik adopts a similar approach of interacting with everyone on the field and not letting the junior players feel left out.

A veteran in the IPL (Indian Premier League) scene, Karthik held the record for maximum dismissals of 131—101 catches and 30 stumpings. Dhoni broke the record in the 2019 IPL final at Hyderabad by taking the catches of

Rohit Sharma and Quinton de Kock—an aggregate of 132 dismissals. Karthik would least rue the fact that he lost the record to one of the greatest icons of the game. If it comes to replacing Dhoni at the World Cup, Karthik would be making his debut at the premier tournament.

Nayan Mongia on Dinesh Karthik

We all know the debate – Karthik or Rishabh Pant. There was more support for Pant because he is young and a dynamite at the crease. But Karthik was preferred because he has the experience that would be much-needed in a tournament as big as the World Cup. True, Karthik has not grabbed the opportunities that came his way. He was inconsistent with his batting and wicketkeeping but he worked on his game and fought his way back. Pant was a great contender for the second wicketkeeper's slot but I felt Karthik had a better chance. At a World Cup, you need experience more than exuberance. Age is on Pant's side and he will get his chance in the future but as of now I feel Karthik is the right choice. It is his last opportunity to grab. If he gets to play I am sure Karthik's experience will be a big plus for the team.

Nayan Mongia did well as a wicketkeeper in two editions of the World Cup—1996 and 1999.

KL Rahul

AGE	26 YEARS
PLAYING ROLE	OPENING BATSMAN
BATTING	RIGHT-HAND BAT
BOWLING	-
ODI MATCHES	14

From a batsman, known to be over-defensive, KL Rahul's transition should be applauded as an attacking stroke player and is a story that reflects the Karnataka cricketer's tremendous ability to adapt and implement. His state coach, J Arun Kumar, has many stories to share but the best is the tale filled with pride about how Rahul learnt the lessons early and quickly.

Arun, who backed the opening batsman to do well at the World Cup, said:

> There is no dearth of talent in Karnataka. Rahul, Karun (Nair), Mayank (Agarwal), Manish (Pandey), Gowtham (K), Shreyas (Gopal) were quick to realise that it was not difficult to play for India. It took hard work and they were willing to bend their back. In Rahul's case, he was not willing to compromise on the schedule that he was given to follow and that helped him make a debut four years after playing his first first-class match.

Rahul was not the aggressive batsman that he comes across now. Arun praised him by stating:

> He was, in fact, defensive. We had a series of talks and I told him he would have to push his scoring rate. The strike rate has to be impressive because captains and coaches like it when you play to win than play to save. Rahul always had the skills to play all the shots you can think of.

Seasoned players in Karnataka were aware of the progress Rahul had made in the junior ranks. He had come through the grind and, as Arun remembered, was ready to play for the country at the end of the second season in domestic cricket. Rahul earned praises from the experts by the manner in which he handled fast bowlers. That he was fearless was well known but his technique and unflinching concentration prepared him well for international cricket.

Two innings that confirmed Rahul's awesome batting prowess came in the Duleep Trophy final against Central Zone at Delhi. Knocks of 185 and 130 saw Rahul rise in stature, but his dominance failed to prevent South Zone's defeat. A star had arrived that day.

Karnataka has a history of producing quality cricketers, from GR Viswanath, BS Chandrasekhar, EAS Prasanna, Syed Kirmani, Roger Binny, Brijesh Patel to the modern era where Rahul Dravid, Anil Kumble, J Srinath, Venkatesh Prasad have played with distinction. The discerning critics are convinced that Rahul has the talent to join that elite list. Binny said:

> Rahul has loads of talent. He must work on his game a bit more. He has to be more consistent because there is intense competition now. I would also like to tell him to be wiser in his approach to batting. He is trying to play too many shots. If he learns to build the innings, like Gavaskar or Dravid, his longevity in cricket will be assured.

Rahul has worked on his temperament. Losing his slot in the team has taught him to put value to his wicket. Binny said:

> You can't go bang-bang at the highest level. I know he is a very intelligent cricketer who can better himself if he begins to read the situation carefully. There is a difference between 50 overs and T20 cricket. In 50 overs, he can play his normal game and accumulate runs.

Having played all three formats of the game has its impact on Rahul. It is evident that he often looks to manufacture shots. Having risen through the ranks, Rahul is aware of his batsmanship. The matting wickets experience in Bangalore has also groomed him to be mentally strong to confront the best of the bowlers.

His parents KN Lokesh and C Rajeshwari have played an important part in his cricket journey. Lokesh, a professor at the National Institute of Technology, and Rajeshwari, who teaches history at Mangalore University, have contrasting approach when it comes to following their son's cricket. Rajeshwari prefers not to watch his batting while Lokesh does not mind rising early to see Rahul at the crease, just like he did when Rahul crafted a century in the 2014 Sydney Test against Australia.

Rahul, however, had a forgettable debut with scores of 3 and 1 at Melbourne but he was again scoring a hundred four innings after Sydney—108 against Sri Lanka at in a winning cause. The Man of the Match went a long way in establishing Rahul as a reliable opener. The biggest backing to Rahul has come from the team management, which has thwarted any attempt by the selectors to exclude him. Rahul is an important factor in the scheme of things planned by Virat Kohli and Ravi Shastri ahead of any series.

Karnataka's rich legacy in cricket has been upheld by Rahul, who can hardly be faulted when it comes to success against strong attacks. Viswanath and Dravid rarely failed when the team needed them to score big and Rahul draws his motivation from them. When he was involved in the controversy of appearing on a TV show which dented his reputation, Rahul lost little time in getting back to work. He was able to gain his focus when he played a few matches for India 'A', where he was able to interact with Dravid in what he can remember as career-saving lessons. 'I spent a lot of time with Dravid, working on my game and chatting about cricket. He helped me a lot in the games I played,' he had remarked in an interview with *The Times of India*.

Four centuries in his first 12 Tests, including a 199 against England at Chennai in 2016, showcased Rahul as the batsman to watch. It is another matter that in his last ten Test innings before the World Cup, he did not register even one half-century. But the World Cup is about limited overs, a format he embraced with a century in his One Day International (ODI) debut against Zimbabwe in 2016. Rahul symbolises the modern batting philosophy where consistency is the key. He has the strike rate and a wide repertoire of strokes to excel on the big stage. The World Cup beckons him to make a strong statement of his batsmanship.

Sandeep Patil on KL Rahul

I consider him as a very exciting batsman. The confidence that he brings to his job speaks for his awesome talent. He has a fantastic range of shots and that makes him a batsman to watch out for. I know there is talk of the English weather and all that but let me make it very clear that all tournaments conducted by the ICC are held in near-perfect conditions.

There could be some clouds sometimes but that should not worry the Indians. Rahul, in particular, should look to play a natural game. I would have been surprised had he not been picked for the World Cup because he has the game to shine in England. Rahul's confidence at the crease is a major factor that will see him through. He should not worry about the conditions at all. They will suit his batting.

Sandeep Patil was a dashing batsman who was part of the team in the 1983 World Cup.

Hardik Pandya

AGE	25 YEARS
PLAYING ROLE	ALLROUNDER
BATTING	RIGHT-HAND BAT
BOWLING	RIGHT-ARM MEDIUM-FAST
ODI MATCHES	45

At the Champions Trophy in 2017, India was taking on its arch-rival Pakistan in a league match at Birmingham. It was important for India to begin its campaign on a winning note. A victory against Pakistan is considered the best tonic for Indian cricket, and it was no different on this occasion too. India won by 124 runs. There was a development, however, which came as a pleasant shock to all those present in the dressing room—Hardik Pandya being asked to pad up ahead of Mahendra Singh Dhoni. This was unthinkable for anyone who follows Indian cricket closely.

It was not that India was struggling. At 285 for three in 46.2 overs, the stage was ideal for Dhoni to walk in and play his attacking game. But coach Anil Kumble had other ideas. Dhoni was padded up but Kumble ordered Pandya to be ready next. The youngster was obviously shocked to be asked to bat ahead of Dhoni, in his eighth One Day International (ODI) match, was going to put him under pressure. Pandya did not let go of the opportunity.

Taking strike in the company of skipper Virat Kohli, Pandya slammed 20 off six balls with three sixes. He had precisely done what Kumble had asked him to—decimate the Pakistan attack. It was a small contribution, which proved to be big in shaping Pandya's career. The knock was his tribute to Dhoni, who was quick to pat him when he returned to the dressing room.

No wonder, Pandya, after Mumbai Indians beat Chennai Super Kings in the 2019 IPL (Indian Premier League) qualifier, posted this message on Twitter: 'My inspiration, my friend, my brother, my legend.' Pandya had always expressed his respect for Dhoni and the influence the veteran had on his cricket. It was a gesture which won Pandya many admirers.

Only a few months ago, he had lost face when he made some disparaging remarks in an interview to Karan Johar in Johar's television show. He faced disciplinarian action from the Board of Control for Cricket in India (BCCI) and learnt a few life lessons. The strong response from the cricket fraternity had an impact on Pandya, who apologised and vowed to transform himself. And he did.

Few know that Kumble was among the first to realise his potential. In fact, Kumble threw a protective shield around Pandya, who was a compulsive stroke player of immense potential. He had the strength to put the ball beyond the boundary and his range of shots meant he was always looking to dominate. Kumble not only encouraged him to play his natural game but also pleaded with critics not to be harsh when judging Pandya's potential.

Coming from Baroda, Pandya, along with his brother Krunal, was a regular at the academy conducted by former India wicketkeeper, Kiran More. More noted:

> He was determined to make it big. It was a grind for him and, sometimes, I realised he was overworking for

his ambition to play for India. But I did never feel like putting shackles on his aspirations. It was the hard work of him as a teenager that went a long way in shaping his game.

Pandya grew in strength once he realised he had the backing of Kohli and Kumble. Even the new coach, Ravi Shastri, saw to it that Pandya was handled well and given the freedom to express himself freely on the field. During India's tour to New Zealand, Shastri praised Pandya by saying, 'He's a natural talent. He is a match-winner.'

He took him seven innings to hit his first ODI half-century. It happened when he batted at no. 7 against England at Kolkata. He was to crack another half-century five matches later—76 against Pakistan at The Oval in the final of the Champions Trophy. The innings came in a losing cause as India collapsed under the pressure of chasing a target of 339. But the innings helped Pandya establish himself firmly in the team as an all-rounder after his consistent spells of medium pace.

He was soon being considered as an all-rounder in Tests too, which was not acceptable to the purists and the experts. Sunil Gavaskar opined, 'You want to call Hardik Pandya an all-rounder? Whoever wants to call Pandya an all-rounder, may call! But I don't think so.' The master was right. Being an all-rounder in Tests demanded skills of a different kind and Pandya was clearly not ready for it. Eleven Tests since his debut against Sri Lanka in 2017 have not been able to convince experts, even though he has a century to his credit.

Pandya's role in the team will be critical. He has the ability to step up the scoring in the late order and often it can dictate the course of the contest. Kapil was adept at pushing the score in the latter half of the innings and Pandya has the same temperament to achieve his targets. He is devastating on flat pitches and would need to adjust his game in England if the ball begins to swing. The swing may not be pronounced when he comes to bat, but the opponents would surely have done their homework on Pandya who loves to have a go at the bowlers.

After losing his place in the team following the Karan Johar TV-show episode, Pandya hit back strongly. According to a report in *India Today*, he told his mentor, Kiran More, 'Sir, I hit a thousand balls in Australia when I was removed.' That was Pandya's way of staying in touch to hit the ball cleanly. It reflected on Pandya's love for the game. He was hurt in his own admission but pledged to reform and ensure he remained a key component in the team.

Pandya's stroke play adds to India's batting depth and his bowling can always be a bonus. 'He is a good bowler who can read the opponent well,' noted More, who has monitored Pandya's progress in cricket—from Baroda to a place in the Mumbai Indians team and finally in the Indian cricket team. Pandya may not be close to Kapil Dev, but he promises to take inspiration from the legendary all-rounder. It augurs well for the team.

Robin Singh on Hardik Pandya

His ability to win the game on his own is superior to anyone in world cricket. There are not many like him. He can smash both fast and spin bowlers with the same ease and confidence that demoralises the opponents in no time. He is exceptionally talented and amazingly explosive with the bat. He has worked on his game, on his temperament, fitness, with the sole aim to excel on the big stage. He is ready now. He has a unique approach because he has realised he can not model his game on someone. His shot selection has a method, which has dramatically improved. The best thing about Hardik is he is not afraid of executing his plans. If he has to tear into the bowling, then he will. He will be the most important man on the field because he can bowl as well. He is going to make a huge impact at the World Cup.

Robin Singh, an all-rounder, figured in the 1999 World Cup.

Bhuvaneshwar Kumar

AGE	29 YEARS
PLAYING ROLE	BOWLER
BATTING	RIGHT-HAND BAT
BOWLING	RIGHT-ARM MEDIUM
ODI MATCHES	105

Fast bowlers are mostly strong, muscular and athletic. The images of Wesley Hall, Joel Garner, Colin Croft, Dennis Lillee, Allan Donald, to name a few, appear menacing when they run in from a distance, pounding the turf and hurling the ball at a great speed. The bounce they generate can rattle the most confident of batsmen. They are known to be fierce competitors, given the nature of their art. 'You don't look at an angry fast bowler in his eyes. It angers him more,' as once remarked by the former India opener, Anshuman Gaekwad. Some Indian batsmen, standing up to West Indian speedster Malcolm Marshall, would look the other way when he would come down the pitch on being denied an appeal or being hit for a boundary.

But Bhuvaneshwar Kumar, the swing bowler from Meerut, is quite an antithesis to the impression most carry of a fast bowler. He is not strongly built but is supremely fit. He is not tall but can generate bounce and speed. He does not lose his composure when attacked. On the other hand, he draws inspiration from the fact that he has to improve to make an impression on the batsman. Often, batsmen see him smiling, which, actually, is a sign that the bowler is plotting his next move.

Bhuvi, as he is fondly called in the cricket circuit, has rarely lost his cool on the field. His long-time coach, Sanjay Rastogi, says:

> It's his character not to get upset. He has always been like this. He loved competing at our centre (Victoria Park) and did not mind a contest where he had to give his best. His discipline and behaviour are two qualities that I have not seen in most cricketers of this generation. For Bhuvi, cricket is a way of life

and he believes in respecting the batsman for his scoring prowess.

Always punctual at the nets, Bhuvi made his mark in the domestic season. It took him five years of domestic grind before he earned a spot in the Indian One Day International (ODI) team. He made a splendid debut against Pakistan at Chennai in 2012, where he claimed two wickets in a tight spell of nine overs. He had justified his elevation to the Indian team and within a year he figured in the Test squad against Australia at the same venue.

The legendary Kapil Dev, a crafty swing bowler himself, classifies Bhuvi as a rhythm bowler. Kapil analysed the seam bowler by stating:

> His strength is his rhythm. He is quick to settle into his rhythm and read the situation to suit his bowling. I like his knuckleball. It unsettles the batsman. It's not easy to bowl but he has come to employ it judiciously. It would have taken me years to learn this craft.

Among the current crop of fast bowlers, Bhuvi stands out for his line and length. His forte is swing but the nagging line that he commands adds to the pressure on the batsmen, especially in ODIs, where the focus is on rotating the strike and picking up boundaries. It is rare to see Bhuvi being clobbered as he backs himself, although he makes errors early in his spells. His ability to recover and regain his rhythm helps the other bowlers also gain confidence.

Bhuvi spends hours in the nets, practising his swing and working on his yorker. As a bowler, he has to constantly focus on improving his art, as wicket-taking is a tough job. Bowlers have to keep on innovating to fox the batsmen and Bhuvi is good at it. A proud Rastogi says:

> Often he would come alone to the coaching centre. Sometimes, he would report within hours after returning from a long tour. Such dedication is the reason why Bhuvi has managed to keep his focus on the game. He is remarkably grounded, despite all the success and fame that he has achieved. It is a sight to see him mingle with other trainees at the coaching centre.

Humility marks his cricket. For Bhuvi, wicket-taking is part of the job. Often, he does not even celebrate his wicket when most bowlers break into a jog on claiming a wicket. There are times when he does express himself and these are the occasions when he would have set up the batsman. 'He is very good at it. To set up a batsman is a great personal victory for a bowler, and I have seen him do this very often,' observed the former Indian seamer, Ashish Nehra.

Bhuvi is a performer in all formats of the game. His probing line plays on the mind of the openers who are looking to establish an early dominance. This is when Bhuvi strikes. He is known to give his team early breakthroughs, a trait that is found in bowlers who are not averse to experiment in the middle. He may not appear to be a normal fast bowler, but Bhuvi, with a supple body, commands respect from some of the biggest hitters of the game.

Bhuvi's swing will be a huge factor in England. The pressure on him is bound to be huge as the team management believes he is the cog in the Indian fast bowling wheel, with Mohammed Shami and Jasprit Bumrah completing the fascinating trio. The captain looks up to Bhuvi in times of distress, when the opponents are on a rampage. More often than not, Bhuvi is able to contain the flow of runs and that makes him a very significant member of India's World Cup campaign.

Playing video games is his favourite vocation when not on the cricket field. It helps him remain sharp and adds to his capacity to out-think the batsmen. He is not someone who displays emotions on the field; Bhuvi's composed nature guides him during tough times. He is the first Indian bowler to have a five-wicket haul in every format of the game. His form at the World Cup will be crucial. A quick wicket or two at the top has been a habit with Bhuvi. He would do well to pull off such acts in England, where the conditions would suit his bowling the most.

Balvinder Sandhu on Bhuvneshwar Kumar

He is a tremendous swing bowler. Natural. His record speaks for him. He lost his rhythm when he tried to put in extra pace. No need to do that. His swing bowling is what makes him a dangerous bowler. Trying for pace can end up with an injury and that would not help the team in a tournament of such importance. He has a great action for a swing bowler, and I want Bhuvi to remember that. He always looks relaxed. To me, it is his forte not to lose his cool when under pressure. He is a smart bowler who is good at setting up a batsman. His resilience will carry the team in the World Cup. He is a fighter from within and a nice guy at heart. If he swings the ball from a length, I am sure he will do very well in England.

Balvinder Sandhu foxed the batsmen with his swing bowling in the 1983 World Cup.

INDIA

Yuzvendra Chahal

AGE	28 YEARS
PLAYING ROLE	BOWLER
BATTING	RIGHT-HAND BAT
BOWLING	LEGBREAK GOOGLY
ODI MATCHES	41

Indian cricket has seen some of the most fascinating leg-spinners, who made a mark at the international cricket with their wily stuff. From Subhash Gupte and BS Chandrasekhar to LS Sivaramakrishnan to Anil Kumble, all unique in their own way. Gupte was a master of the flight and was good at snaring batsmen with his variety. So was Sivaramakrishnan, who, however, did not achieve his potential. Chandrasekhar and Kumble made a huge impact with their styles. Many could not make to the highest grade, but in times, when the shorter formats of the game have come to add excitement, the emergence of Yuzvendra Chahal has augured well for the team. He has not played a Test yet but made enough waves in limited overs cricket to earn a place in the Indian team for the World Cup.

Jind, one of the oldest districts in Haryana, is not known for cricket but Chahal has put it on the international map by making his presence known with some outstanding performances for India. He brings old-world charm to his game with his measured and composed approach to the game. The studious look on his face reflects his cricket—no room for pressure and a certain level of diligence—where he is always looking to take on the best. Chahal is known to challenge himself in situations where he motivates himself to win the one-on-one combats with the best of batsmen. A spinner's best weapon is his temperament when confronted by a batsman who looks to dominate, and Chahal has the qualities to remain in control of the task given to him.

He is a spinner who loves to take wickets and not bowl the restrictive line. Every time the captain tosses the ball to him, Chahal gears up to accept the responsibility. The sparkle in his eyes at the possibility of breaching the defence of the batsman is an indication that he has detected a possible way to win the battle. This trait comes to him from his initial love for chess, a game where he represented India in Asian Youth and World Youth Championships. His name figures in the official site of FIDE (World Chess Federation).

Chahal was rated as a highly promising chess player with a philosophy pure and simple—to decimate the opponent. Unable to find sponsors for his travels to chess tournaments, Chahal focussed on cricket, trying his hand as a medium-pacer, before settling down to bowl leg spin. He has grown into a fearless bowler and it is important for a spinner to accept punishment as part of the job. In the era gone by, bowlers would not mind applauding a good shot by the batsmen. Not anymore.

He is an integral part of the Indian bowling, whose pace and spin are in perfect proportion. Chahal complements the efforts of Kuldeep Yadav and Ravindra Jadeja by exploring different angles. It is not always possible for him to shackle the batsmen but Chahal enjoys the fight in the middle. It is a mind game; not quite like the ones he waged on the chessboard but certainly with the determination that a winner brings to the arena.

Chahal's serious foray into cricket began in 2002 when he played for Haryana in the Polly Umrigar (U-15) Trophy.

He made a modest start with just one wicket to his name. In the same season, he had his first encounter with Virat Kohli, who slammed a brilliant 70. Three years later, Chahal and Kohli faced each other again in the Vijay Merchant (U-17) Trophy. Chahal was still playing age-group tournaments when Kohli made his international debut with an One Day International (ODI) against Sri Lanka at Dambulla in 2008.

Chahal's first-class debut was unimpressive as he went wicketless against Madhya Pradesh in the Ranji Trophy match at Indore in the 2009–2010 season. He continued to toil in the Ranji Trophy before getting his big break to play for Mumbai Indians (MI) in the 2011 Champions League, where he got to bowl in the company of Lasith Malinga and Harbhajan Singh. His appearances in first-class cricket became fewer but he made his Indian Premier League (IPL) debut in 2013 for MI against Kolkata Knight Riders.

The IPL shifted to Dubai in 2009 due to General Elections in the country and Chahal too found a new team—Royal Challengers Bangalore (RCB). He has remained loyal to RCB and in the process struck a bonding with Kohli, which helped his cricket to grow. The experience gained at RCB and the opportunity to prosper under Kohli's captaincy paved the way for his international debut in 2016—playing in the ODI and T20 series against Zimbabwe. His career took off from that overseas tour and Chahal became an essential part of the Indian attack.

Confidence plays an important part in any professional sportsman's career and Chahal continued to develop his bowling strength. He had the full support of Kohli. He gives credit to MS Dhoni for encouraging the bowlers. In a recent interview to *The Hindu*, he said:

> I usually bowl the ninth or the tenth over. By this time, Mahi *bhai* (Dhoni) gets a fair idea of the pitch and he shares it with me. Virat *bhaiya* gives me the field that I have in mind before suggesting changes. In short, I remain focused on what I have to do and not think too much about the pitch and field placements of a particular batsman.

His priorities are clear. To attack and follow the instructions given by his seniors. Former India seamer Ashish Nehra observed, 'He is a smart cricketer, thanks to his grooming in chess (where he has a National age-group title) and is always smiling.'

Chahal's spell of six for 42 against Australia at Melbourne, in the 2019 tour, is a special show in his career. It was the first time a spinner had taken six wickets in an

ODI in Australia as Chahal ran through the opposition. He bowled every possible delivery that a leg-spinner can pull out of his stock. In his interactions with fellow cricketers on Chahal TV, a chat show invented by the Board of Control for Cricket in India (BCCI), he comes off as a host who is well prepared. His homework for the chat show is exemplary, as he lights up the light-hearted episodes. He is confident about excelling at the World Cup and the team expects him to keep that promise.

L Sivaramakrishnan on Yuzvendra Chahal

I am always delighted when a leg-spinner finds a place in the team. Not that the other styles of spinners do not make me happy, but a leg-spinner brings in a variety that can be very tough to handle. I find Yuzvendra a very useful and intelligent bowler with some superb variations. A spinner has to have variations when bowling and it would be a really formidable challenge at the World Cup. I have followed him closely and can say with a certain confidence that he is among the rare ones who can set up the batsman. My only complaint against him is that there is too much of leg-stump attack, which can make his googly an identifiable ball. He must also explore the off-stump line to fox the batsman. He can do that in style. He has to make the batsman go for the cover drive because it can be a wicket-taking ball.

L Sivaramakrishnan, who played in the 1987 World Cup, was a wily leg-spinner.

Mohammed Shami

AGE	28 YEARS
PLAYING ROLE	BOWLER
BATTING	RIGHT-HAND BAT
BOWLING	RIGHT-ARM FAST-MEDIUM
ODI MATCHES	63

Mohammed Shami's success story is as much a tale of valour and dedication as it is a telling commentary on the system that prevails in Uttar Pradesh. Shami, hailing from Sahaspur, played all his competitive cricket for Bengal. All because his father, Tousif Ali, who knew the system in Uttar Pradesh very well. He could not trust the officials to encourage a youngster who had no godfather. Shami would have ended up attending one selection trial after another in Lucknow or Meerut, watching least-deserving candidates make it to the state junior teams. Hence, his father decided to put him on a train to Kolkata to enable Shami to chase his dreams in the City of Joy. It was a decision that gave Indian cricket a fast bowler who had searing pace and a passion to bowl untiringly at both nets and matches.

In Kolkata, Shami was fortunate to come into contact with Debabrata Das, who ran the Town Club. It was a decent club where Shami got to play regularly and, importantly, Das gave him shelter at his home since Shami had no place to stay. Many years later, Das helped Shami buy a flat in the city when the boy from Sahaspur made an impact at the international stage with his bowling. Das also showed excellent spirit by letting Shami play for Mohun Bagan. Club politics dictated the move since Shami needed a club with a strong voice to push for his selection in the higher grade. Not that Shami needed such favours. His pace was making heads turn at Maidan in Kolkata and he was talked about with respect in Kolkata's cricket circle.

Shami was living his father's dream. Ali, who dealt in spare parts for tractors, knew a thing or two about fast bowling since he was one. The father also could see the spark in his son and did not waste any time in encouraging the lad. Sahaspur, a dusty town near Moradabad with little cricket facilities, was not the place for his son to pursue cricket; Kolkata was the right destination. Ali and his family pat themselves for the move to back Shami, who was hardly 16 when he left home to compete in Kolkata's cricket maidans. Shami's coach, Badruddin Siddiqui, who was running a centre in Moradabad, also supported the idea of the boy looking for avenues outside Uttar Pradesh.

Kolkata welcomed Shami with open arms. Support came from many quarters and a place in the state team for the CK Nayudu (U-22) Trophy in 2009 was well earned. His journey had begun and his family back home felt relieved and happy for Shami, who, at 19, had taken the early steps to build a career in cricket. In the next season, he graduated to make his first-class debut against Assam and picked three wickets. One of the umpires, AN Kishore, a medium-pacer himself, was impressed with Shami's ability to generate pace.

Interestingly, the media took some time to get his name correct. They called him Mohammad Shami, Shami Mohammed, Shami Ahmed. He was not losing sleep over this identity issue. He kept on performing till the critics got his name right as he made his One Day International (ODI) debut against Pakistan at Delhi in 2013, opening the bowling with distinction in India's 10-run victory. The celebrations in Sahaspur were understandable for Shami had earned the India cap after figuring in ten first-class matches for Bengal.

Sambaran Banerjee, the former Bengal wicketkeeper, also played an important role in recognising Shami's talent. Banerjee was instrumental in giving Sourav Ganguly a break and, as a state selector, had picked Shami in the under-22 team. Banerjee said:

> He is a rare talent. I saw him in a local league match and he bowled like a champion. I was impressed with his pace, the seam position and the bounce he got off the pitch. His outswinger, at a speed of 140-plus, looked lethal too. I saw him in the morning and the same evening I picked him up and included in the team. Imagine, this boy would play club cricket for Rs 100 a day, sharing a room with four others in Howrah. His journey to the Indian team is an amazing and very inspiring story.

Shami's progress was steady even though he was troubled by injuries at various stages. He once failed a fitness test but every time he came back with a roar. His Test debut against the West Indies in 2013, at the iconic Eden Gardens, was sensational. It was Sachin Tendulkar's farewell series and

Shami claimed nine wickets in the match as India won by an innings. There was high praise for Shami. He could not have asked for a better debut as some of his colleagues from the Town Club and Mohun Bagan watched him from the stands. India had found a reliable opening bowler who could hustle the best of batsmen.

For Chetan Sharma, who played the 1987 World Cup and took a hat-trick against New Zealand at Nagpur, the sight of Shami bowling is 'heartening' and impactful on the game. He observed:

> I have not seen a bowler with such a brilliant seam position. His wrist position is a dream for any fast bowler, and it is such a delight to follow the ball into the wicketkeeper's gloves. You can see the upright seam clearly and most batsmen would agree that he is a very difficult bowler to face. The fact that he manages to swing the ball at that pace is another plus point. If only he could work on his yorkers, Shami would be a complete fast bowler. He is going to be the most important factor in India's campaign at the World Cup.

Shami's experience at the 2015 World Cup, where he picked 17 wickets, should help him when he will bowl in England. He had played that tournament despite a knee injury. This time, he is fit and bowling with splendid rhythm. With Jasprit Bumrah as his company, they forms the most effective fast-bowling pair in the World Cup. India can expect heroics from him. He is good with a new ball and better with an old one.

Venkatesh Prasad on Mohammed Shami

He is an absolutely brilliant bowler. His seam position is flawless, a bowler's delight actually. His outswingers can leave you in a trance because he tends to hit the right length with the right speed. He is good when he bowls back of the length ball. I have always been impressed with his line on the off and the fourth stump. It keeps the batsman guessing. To me, he is the stroke bowler that India needs at the World Cup. The best thing is, it looks like he will take wickets. He has the attitude of a fast bowler. Of course, the expectations from him would be high and I am sure he will love the conditions. He should be motivated by his performances even on flat decks. He must focus on moving the ball and not worry about the end result. He is a match-winner, who I am sure will shine at the World Cup.

Venkatesh Prasad, a crafty seamer, plotted Pakistan's defeat in 1996 and 1999 World Cups.

INDIA

Jasprit Bumrah

AGE	25 YEARS
PLAYING ROLE	BOWLER
BATTING	RIGHT-HAND BAT
BOWLING	RIGHT-ARM FAST-MEDIUM
ODI MATCHES	49

Only a few backed this wiry lad from Ahmedabad to become one of the feared bowlers in international cricket. His action was a point of debate among the experts. 'He would only invite injuries if he continues to bowl like this at the international level,' a former teammate of his had commented in private. This was just about the time when Bumrah was making waves with his bowling, the weird action making him the man in news.

A short run-up was the reason for coaches to discuss Bumrah. He would run in from a small distance and generate scorching pace. The bouncer or the yorker came with tremendous velocity. In later years, he added the slow yorker to his repertoire. He was not the traditional fast bowler, who would mark a long run-up, come thundering in, pound the ball with much of the force exerted by the shoulder, ending his follow through within handshaking distance from the batsman. A glare would complete the act. But not for Bumrah.

He kind of suppresses a smile as he reaches the top of the bowling run-up. Sometimes, he does not even go all the way to the mark. As if by instinct, he would cut short his run-up and let the ball go by putting all his weight behind the delivery. It makes for a delightful sight—from the point of release to his athletic finish and the controlled joy to celebrate a wicket. It defines his personality. The course of the delivery remains an intrigue as Bumrah packs in a change of pace, line and length to bemuse the batsman.

Bumrah was hardly seven when he lost his father. The sad development in the family put the burden of the entire family on his mother's shoulder. She was initially apprehensive, but thanks to her for allowing Bumrah to chase his cricket dreams. There were hardly any facilities but Bumrah had made up his mind to seek a career in cricket. To his good fortune, former New Zealand captain John Wright, when spotting talent for Mumbai Indians, was quick to recognise his potential. It also helped Bumrah that Glenn McGrath, the Australian with one of the best actions for a fast bowler, appreciated his unique action and suggested a few tips too.

Kapil Dev graciously admitted that he had made a mistake initially when asked to analyse the Gujarat speedster. He said:

> I was doubtful because of his strange action. From a short run-up, using his shoulder predominantly to generate pace, he was getting a speed of 140-plus. To me, it was astonishing really. India has found a superb bowler who can use the new and the old ball so well. I love watching him.

Bumrah has an admirer in Chetan Sharma—the former fast bowler with a hat-trick to his name in the 1987 World Cup. In the match against New Zealand at Nagpur, Chetan took the wickets of Ken Rutherford, Ian Smith and Ewen Chatfield to record the first hat-trick in a World Cup match. In the same contest, Sunil Gavaskar hit his only One Day

International (ODI) century as India beat New Zealand for the second time.

Chetan was not the typical fast bowler. He was neither tall nor strong. But he was muscular and used his shoulder to get the ball to kick. His bouncer, like Bumrah's, was deceptive. According to Chetan, Bumrah 'is an exceptional bowler. Very different because of his action but so consistent. The team can bank on him to give breakthroughs. He is a key bowler in all conditions.'

Bumrah has excelled in all the formats of the game. He was at his best in India's three overseas victories in 2018. Against South Africa, in tandem with Bhuvaneshwar, he finished with seven wickets for the Test as India won in style. At Trent Bridge, his five-wicket haul in the second innings set up the massive Indian win against England. Six wickets in the Adelaide Test against Australia showed Bumrah in excellent form and he continued his good work at Melbourne during year end—this time winning the Man of the Match award for his six wickets in the first innings and three in the second. This was the Bumrah visualised by the coaches at the National Cricket Academy and the MRF Pace Foundation, where he had learnt the fine points of bowling.

It is the yorker that makes Bumrah such a fascinating bowler to watch. The great Pakistan fast bowlers, Wasim Akram and Waqar Younis, were known to fire yorkers at will, the ball searing in from different angles, leaving the batsmen in no position to block the rocket. In different situations, Bumrah has proved to be the man to go to for his captain. 'It takes heart to accept challenges so frequently. Obviously, Bumrah has this high level of confidence but his skills also count. The change of pace, the line that he explores and his vicious yorker make Bumrah a difficult bowler to face,' said Venkatesh Prasad.

When Mahendra Singh Dhoni remarked that he was the find of the tour in Australia in 2015, it may have surprised the critics. Just the tonic that Bumrah needed, he used the praise from Dhoni to his benefit, worked on his bowling, where long spells were the preferred choice, and, within a season, he had grown in stature.

Among the many fast bowlers who made it to the Indian team since the retirement of Zaheer Khan, Ashish Nehra and Munaf Patel, he emerged to be the most reliable wicket-taker. A match-winner in his own way, Bumrah has proved to grow from experience. In this team, he is the first choice as a fast bowler and the fact that he can shine on any surface makes him the captain's favourite.

At other times, Bumrah has acknowledged the lessons learnt from the domestic circuit. He would not miss a match for Gujarat. As the former Indian seamer Ajit Agarkar observed, 'Bumrah makes a big difference to the attack,' the team knows this too well.

Madan Lal on Jasprit Bumrah

Honestly, I never thought he would survive international cricket with his action. He was different and that has helped him all the way. It is difficult to pick his ball because of this very different action. He can produce such a pace that can rattle even a well-set batsman. He brings the ball in and that is a huge advantage. He also has a lethal bouncer. I think he is a complete fast bowler and a great asset to India's bowling. He will have a crucial role to play since I know the spinners may not be able to extract much from the pitches in England. Spinners can be effective if the seamers make the early dents, and here Jasprit has a big part to play. He has to provide the early breakthroughs. He has been bowling well. To me, he could well be the bowler to watch at the World Cup.

Madan Lal, a good all-rounder, is best known for taking Viv Richards' wicket in the 1983 World Cup final.

Ravindra Jadeja

AGE	30 YEARS
PLAYING ROLE	ALLROUNDER
BATTING	LEFT-HAND BAT
BOWLING	SLOW LEFT-ARM ORTHODOX
ODI MATCHES	151

Ten years of international cricket have, at various times, proved Ravindra Jadeja's value to the Indian team in all formats of the game. When Kapil Dev called him 'the most valued cricketer' five years ago, he was being generous in his praise of Jadeja. 'His fielding standards have inspired his teammates and it is always nice to see such players who can win a match with his batting, bowling and sometimes with fielding too,' Kapil has said.

Coming from the greatest Indian cricketer, the words worked as magic and Jadeja grew in strength as an all-rounder of merit.

Few backed this left-hander from Rajkot. His debut in 2009, in an One Day International (ODI) against Sri Lanka, was the culmination of a fine run in junior cricket, where he was termed as a bits-and-pieces player. He was, however, one of the youngsters who had the backing of the national selectors. It was generally observed by people who matter in Indian cricket that Jadeja had the potential to develop into a decent all-rounder in limited overs cricket.

Hailing from a modest background, Jadeja had resolved to pursue a career in cricket. Saurashtra, his home state, was not the best of cricket forces in the country but improved facilities meant that there was hope for the likes of Jadeja to dream of an India cap. It was a long grind, but he eventually made it because National selector Raja Venkat had faith in his abilities. Venkat recalled:

> We were looking for an all-rounder to bring balance to the team and Jadeja appeared to be the best candidate. He could bat, bowl and field. He took time to evolve but we never had any doubts that he is the man. When I see him in the team for the World Cup, my thoughts

go back to the time when few backed him to excel at the international stage.

For Jadeja, it has been a journey of trying to convince the captain and the selectors that he belonged to the international circuit. True, his domestic heroics should have established him as a reliable cricketer. He scored triple centuries in first-class cricket and his comeback in 2015–2016 was sensational as Jadeja claimed five wickets or more on six successive occasions. It was a dream run for Jadeja—six for 27 and five for 45 against Tripura, six for 71 and seven for 55 against Jharkhand, six for 75 and seven for 60 against Hyderabad—all on Rajkot's dusty bowl, which was specially prepared to facilitate his comeback to the Indian team.

There was criticism when he was picked for the home Test series against England in the 2012–2013 series. But he justified the break with the wickets of Jonathan Trott and Kevin Pietersen, both deceived by the ball which did not turn. He was termed as a 'dart' bowler than a spinner but Jadeja took the criticism in his stride and drew inspiration from the two big wickets that came his way on the Test debut. He cinched a place in the squad with some decisive performances in the subsequent series against Australia, accounting for Michael Clarke's wicket five times in the first three Tests of the series.

Jadeja looked like a different player from that comeback against South Africa in the 2015 home series. He has been able to assert himself with the bat, which was always considered an asset for the team. Coming late in the order, he has played a number of match-winning innings that have allowed Jadeja to play his natural game. His captains, Mahendra Singh Dhoni and Virat Kohli, have acknowledged Jadeja's ability to hit boundaries and sixes at will in critical situations.

As Venkat pointed out, 'He was considered initially only for his potential in one-day cricket. He was an accurate bowler and would fire the ball in rather than spin it. His batting in home conditions was exceptional, which made him an integral part of the one-day squad.' But he nearly lost his confidence at the end of an ODI against England when he got the flak for not finishing the game despite a fine 87. He was crestfallen but the selectors spoke to him and boosted Jadeja's confidence as he recovered from the criticism.

The biggest break, as Jadeja once remarked, was the Afro-Asia under-19 Asia Cup at Visakhapatnam in November 2005. It gave his cricketing dreams a boost and he figured in a number of limited overs tournament at the junior level. The regular competition enabled him to grow as a cricketer by imbibing the finer points of batting, learning to play within his limitations and making the most of the opportunities that came his way. He had the example of Mohammad Kaif, who had his limitations but strengthened his place in the team with the help of his exceptional fielding.

The golden ball that he won at the Champions Trophy in 2013 was one of his finest achievements on the field. He was the Man of the Match in the final, where wickets of Ian Bell and Trott at critical stages of the second half paved the way for India to win. The tournament was a T20 affair, rather than the normal 50 overs a side, and it helped India since the tournament had players who were adept at the shortest format of the game. When the Champions Trophy returned to England four years later, the old format was restored and Pakistan won the title with a rousing win against India in the final.

What works in Jadeja's favour is that he knows how to hang in—be it bowling or batting. He can pull off a magical act in the field to underline his utility to the team. He is in the thick of the action on the field and he loves every moment of it, even if it means sprinting from the boundary to give the bowler a celebratory hug. Neither a classical spinner in the truest sense nor an attractive batsman, but

Jadeja can emerge as a dominant force in India's campaign at the World Cup.

Piyush Chawla on Ravindra Jadeja

It is in the interest of Indian cricket that he should make a comeback to the one-day squad. He has all the qualities that make him the formidable cricketer that he is. His batting complements his bowling and the fact that he is an exceptional fielder in any position makes him an asset to the team. His bowling has improved big time from the time I have first seen him. He is a genuine all-rounder and adds value to the team. He can perform with the ball even on unresponsive pitches and he will be handy with the bat at no. 7 or 8. I would want him to stick to the basics in England, just like Virat, who plays normal strokes even in pressure situations. There is no need for him to get overawed as he has the experience of having played in the last World Cup. He is a complete package.

Piyush Chawla, an impressive leg-spinner, earned glory in the 2011 World Cup win.

INDIA

Kuldeep Yadav

AGE	24 YEARS
PLAYING ROLE	BOWLER
BATTING	LEFT-HAND BAT
BOWLING	SLOW LEFT-ARM CHINAMAN
ODI MATCHES	44

Kanpur was once called the Manchester of India. It was famous for its textile and leather industries. Sports, cricket in particular, was not part of the culture in this dusty city, although the Green Park Stadium was a permanent Test venue. The emergence of Sports School in Kanpur attracted the youth to look at a career in sports. The city got its first Test cricketer in Gopal Sharma, an off-spinner who played five Tests and 11 One Day Internationals (ODIs).

He was a kind of motivation for cricketers in a state that was considered to be an insignificant part of the Indian cricket circuit. In later years, players like Shashikant Khandkar, Suresh Raina, Mohammad Kaif, Piyush Chawla, RP Singh and Bhuvneshwar Kumar made Uttar Pradesh proud.

For Kuldeep Yadav, there was no legacy to follow. The facilities to pursue cricket were poor and he had to toil. It was not easy to catch the attention of the selectors since the competition was tough and the state was notorious for ignoring talents. When Yadav was trying to make a mark, a young cricketer had jumped off a building in protest. The cricketer was not chosen in the under-15 team. Yadav was distraught when the same fate befell him. Yadav was only 13 and his family was concerned with the boy's future. His parents and three sisters backed him to achieve his goal and he found himself on track soon.

Kapil Pandey, his coach at Rovers Academy, never had any doubt about this special talent. The fact that he admired Pakistan's great bowler, Wasim Akram, showed his bent of mind to become a bowler. The coach persuaded the kid to try his hand at spin. The difference was that Yadav was unique, bowling Chinaman, which means a ball that spins from off to leg, bowled by a left-handed bowler to a right-handed batsman. He was quite an unorthodox bowler, who was bound to make an impression on his opponents because of his style.

Paul Adams, the mysterious South African bowler, and Australia's Brad Hogg have been the modern practitioners of the wrist spin, turning the ball viciously to the right-handers. Pandey was pleasantly surprised by Yadav's action and he accepted the challenge of nurturing the boy. It was 2004. Gradually, Yadav picked up the basics of the game and modelled himself on Shane Warne, who was a modern great. Warne's wrist work became an obsession for Yadav. After three years, from the time he came to Pandey for coaching, he finally made it to the state under-15 team to play the Polly Umrigar Trophy.

In his first competitive match for Uttar Pradesh, Yadav made a brilliant 43 and claimed four wickets to justify his selection. His dreams had taken wings and the next year he earned a slot in the state under-16 team for the Vinoo Mankad Trophy. His progress was steady before big-time cricket summoned Yadav, who played for India under-19 team (Townsville Quadrangular Series in 2012) even before making his first-class debut. He was part of the India under-19 team for the Top End Series in 2013 in Australia and an under-19 Quadrangular series at home the same year. The boy from a modest background, living on the outskirts of Kanpur, had finally arrived. He was on his way to earn glory at the big stage.

He was picked by Mumbai Indians in 2012 and that gave the 'Chinaman' the confidence of achieving success in cricket. Things were looking up for Yadav, who once almost gave up the game in disgust. His family and coach stood strongly behind him and the doors to international cricket opened in 2014 when he was selected for the ICC under-19 World Cup in Dubai. He was yet to play a first-class match though. A stint with Kolkata Knight Riders in the 2014 Champions League meant he was on the right path. He was able to interact with Akram, his hero from the formative years in cricket. In the same season, he made his first-class debut—Ranji Trophy match against Madhya Pradesh at Indore. Four wickets in the only innings he bowled was a decent start for his career.

Yadav deserved his Test debut against Australia at Dharamsala when coach Anil Kumble picked him to take the slot of an injured Virat Kohli. The stand-in captain, Ajinkya Rahane, kept his faith in the lad who responded splendidly, taking four wickets for 68 runs, including the well-set David Warner. He rattled the middle-order with the wickets of Peter Handscomb and Glenn Maxwell to trigger an Australian collapse. He got to bowl just five overs in the second innings but the 'Chinaman' had already made a huge impact. The lad from Kanpur was now a certainty in the Indian Test squad. He toured the West Indies and Sri Lanka and played against New Zealand and Sri Lanka at home.

Former Uttar Pradesh left-arm spinner Rajindar Singh Hans, who was the state selector when Yadav was making his mark, recalled fondly of Yadav's 'dedication' and ability to learn. Hans said:

> He was different as we all could see. I remember telling him once to go and stay at the wicket and he obliged by digging himself in. It showed his discipline even though he was not very happy with his batting. He would not concede an inch to the batsman and was fiercely competitive. His accuracy has been a rare quality because his style makes it extremely difficult.

Yadav is a determined spinner who understands the importance of consistency. He is not averse to flighting the ball and his change of pace often hustles the batsmen into committing mistakes. A favourite of coach Ravi Shastri, he has come to earn the respect of Kohli too. The captain treats him as his trump card and Yadav too lives up to the expectations. He is considered a match-winner and an impact bowler. This is not bad for a cricketer who almost gave up the game because he was not picked in the state's under-15 team. He is now making waves on the international stage and is an important part of the team's spin strength at the World Cup.

Venkatapathy Raju on Kuldeeep Yadav

He will be your match-winner. Some critics may have remarked about his bowling in the Indian Premier League (IPL) but it was a welcome fatigue. It allowed him to rest his body and mind and concentrate on the job ahead. To me, he is going to be the key component in India's bowling.

Most batsmen would struggle to pick his googly, and he must exploit this advantage. I am very impressed with his variety and control. As he is going to play away from home, it will help him. Like a good spinner, he is able to absorb the punishment and hit back strongly. He should stick to his natural line and look to strike a good rhythm. He is a rhythm bowler. He may get initially anxious because of the big stage but would soon realise it is better not to try too much. With Chahal, he forms an awesome spin pair.

Venkatapathy Raju, with his skillful left-arm spin, played the World Cup in 1992 and 1996.

Ravi Shastri

He has been a cricketing phenomenon. A player turned commentator and now the head coach of the team, which prides itself as a unit that can stun the best on this planet. For Ravi Shastri, life has revolved around cricket, and the former India captain insists that he is still a 'student' of the game.

Drafted into the team in 1981 as a cover for an injured Dilip Doshi, the lanky Shastri made a decent debut against New Zealand and went on to become a regular in the Indian team. He would have hardly imagined the change in fortunes when he was playing the Ranji Trophy quarter-final against Uttar Pradesh in Kanpur, where he got a 'pair' before being asked to join the Indian team in New Zealand. His batting abilities earned him a slot in the one-day squad too and within two years of his Test debut, he managed to force his way into the Indian team for the 1983 World Cup, where he got to play only five matches.

Shastri was the toast of Indian cricket in 1985, when he shut all his critics with a clinical show at the World Championship of Cricket in Australia. With consistent all-round success, he was adjudged Champion of Champions—a tag that sat on him well despite the reputation of not being a quick scorer. Only a few months before the World Cup, he had produced a scintillating 200 with 13 sixes—six of them coming in an over from the Baroda left-arm spinner, Tilak Raj. Shastri was a perfect example of grit and determination making up for the lack of natural talent. He was the most hard-working player of his time, working on his abilities to make runs and take wickets in all formats of the game.

Starting his career at no. 10, Shastri climbed the order to open the innings against England at Manchester in 1982. It was the most forgettable start. After being on the field for more than two days, Shastri opened the innings with Sunil Gavaskar and lasted a mere seven balls. Gavaskar, aware of Shastri's potential, persisted with him as an opener in the next Test at The Oval, and the lanky youngster assumed the reputation of an all-rounder with an innings of 66 against an attack that included Bob Willis, Ian Botham, Paul Allott, Derek Pringle and Phil Edmonds. The knock spoke of his character to fight. Out of his 11 centuries, four came as an opener, the last being a 206 against Australia at Sydney in

1992. He was to play four more Tests before announcing his retirement.

Two years after quitting international cricket at the age of 30 and five months after leading Bombay to a Ranji Trophy title, Shastri took his first step into the world of broadcasting, signing a contract with WorldTel for the Singer World Series at Colombo in September 1994. He made an official announcement to retire from active cricket in Colombo and slipped into the role of a commentator with consummate ease. It was not an overnight development for Shastri to take to the mike. For years, he had dreamt of assuming the role, having heard greats like Richie Benaud, John Arlott and Alan McGilvray and Anant Setalvad—his personal favourites. Shastri would imitate these great voices from the cricket field and soon enjoyed a niche following with his inimitable style.

His immense experience of playing the game helped Shastri establish himself as an analyst in the studio. He rubbed shoulders with the finest in the game and earned respect in little time for his candid opinion on the players and the game. Shastri became an inseparable part of the broadcasting time wherever India played. It gave him a ring-side view of the team and also kept in constant touch with the players, alongside some of whom he had played. He also had stints at the National Cricket Academy and was also part of the Governing Council of the Indian Premier League (IPL).

When the opportunity to coach the Indian team arrived, Shastri accepted the responsibility. He was a stop-gap coach of the team in 2007 for the tour to Bangladesh before returning as the team director from August 2014 to March 2016. He could take pride in India's One Day International (ODI) Series triumph in England in 2014, winning a Test series in Sri Lanka after 22 years in 2015, smashing Australia 3–0 in T20 series in Australia and winning the Asia Cup in 2016. The team reached the semi-finals of the 2015 World Cup and the 2016 T20 World Cup before Anil Kumble took over the role in June 2016.

India won 22 out of 35 matches in Kumble's tenure, but his rocky relationship with skipper Virat Kohli brought his stint to a premature end. Both Kumble and Shastri applied for the job and a debate raged in the cricket world. Shastri was handed the job back a year after he had been removed from the post.

The historic 2018–2019 series win in Australia was Shastri's precious gift to Indian cricket fans. True to his character, he did not hold himself back in giving more importance to Test cricket over his limited overs achievements:

> I'll tell you how satisfying it was for me—World Cup 83 and World Championship 85. This (Test cricket) is as big, or even bigger, because this is the truest format of the game. This is not a team of gods or demigods or seniors or juniors. This is an Indian cricket team that will jump off a cliff to win a game for the country. That is the determination, the ruthlessness, the mindset with which this team went to play in this series and hats off to them to show that courage.

Indians would like to believe that the team would retain the tenacity and flair when it travels to the World Cup. Having missed the chance in 2015, Shastri can give his best in the dressing room, where he is more than a guide and mentor—a friend, as he often tells them. A World Cup title may tempt Shastri to continue. If not, be prepared to listen to his firebrand commentary, for you cannot keep him away from cricket.

World Cup 2019 Fixtures and Matches to Look Out For

Date	Time	Venue	Teams
30 May	3:00 pm	London	Eng vs SA
31 May	**3:00 pm**	**Nottingham**	**Pak vs WI**
01 June	3:00 pm	Cardiff	NZ vs SL
01 June	6:00 pm	Bristol	Afg vs Aus
02 June	3:00 pm	London	BDesh vs SA
03 June	3:00 pm	Nottingham	Eng vs Pak
04 June	3:00 pm	Cardiff	Afg vs SL
05 June	**3:00 pm**	**Southampton**	**Ind vs SA**
05 June	6:00 pm	London	BDesh vs NZ
06 June	**3:00 pm**	**Nottingham**	**Aus vs WI**
07 June	3:00 pm	Bristol	Pak vs SL
08 June	3:00 pm	Cardiff	Eng vs BDesh
08 June	6:00 pm	Taunton	Afg vs NZ
09 June	**3:00 pm**	**London**	**Aus vs Ind**
10 June	3:00 pm	Southampton	SA vs WI
11 June	3:00 pm	Bristol	BDesh vs SL
12 June	**3:00 pm**	**Taunton**	**Aus vs Pak**
13 June	**3:00 pm**	**Nottingham**	**Ind vs NZ**
14 June	3:00 pm	Southampton	Eng vs WI
15 June	3:00 pm	London	Aus vs SL
15 June	6:00 pm	Cardiff	Afg vs SA
16 June	**3:00 pm**	**Manchester**	**Ind vs Pak**

Date	Time	Venue	Teams
17 June	3:00 pm	Taunton	BDesh vs WI
18 June	**3:00 pm**	**Manchester**	**Afg vs Eng**
19 June	**3:00 pm**	**Birmingham**	**NZ vs SA**
20 June	3:00 pm	Nottingham	Aus vs BDesh
21 June	3:00 pm	Leeds	Eng vs SL
22 June	**3:00 pm**	**Southampton**	**Afg vs Ind**
22 June	6:00 pm	Manchester	NZ vs WI
23 June	**3:00 pm**	**London**	**Pak vs SA**
24 June	3:00 pm	Southampton	Afg vs BDesh
25 June	**3:00 pm**	**London**	**Eng vs Aus**
26 June	3:00 pm	Birmingham	NZ vs Pak
27 June	**3:00 pm**	**Manchester**	**Ind vs WI**
28 June	3:00 pm	Chester-le-Street	SA vs SL
29 June	3:00 pm	Leeds	Afg vs Pak
29 June	**6:00 pm**	**London**	**Aus vs NZ**
30 June	**3:00 pm**	**Birmingham**	**Eng vs Ind**
01 July	3:00 pm	Chester-le-Street	SL vs WI
02 July	**3:00 pm**	**Birmingham**	**BDesh vs Ind**
03 July	3:00 pm	Chester-le-Street	Eng vs NZ
04 July	3:00 pm	Leeds	Afg vs WI
05 July	**6:00 pm**	**London**	**BDesh vs Pak**
05 July	**3:00 pm**	**Leeds**	**Ind vs SL**
06 July	**6:00 pm**	**Manchester**	**Aus vs SA**
09 July	3:00 pm	Manchester	1st Semi-final
11 July	3:00 pm	Birmingham	2nd Semi-final
14 July	3:00 pm	London	Final

* Do not miss the highlighted matches.

Acknowledgements

My heartfelt thanks to Paul Vinay Kumar, Jyoti Mehrotra and Rajbilochan Prasad, who worked equally hard to ensure that the book was published in time for the World Cup. Rajiv Beri, MD, Bloomsbury India, for his constant encouragement and support.

Suresh Nambath, Editor, *The Hindu*, and KC Vijaya Kumar, Sports Editor, *The Hindu*, for giving me permission to go ahead with this project.

Thanks are due to many others, notably Austin Coutinho, the extraordinary illustrator, for responding to every request with warmth; dear friend Ghaus Mohammad for supporting whatever I attempt.

My wonderful family, wife Sunanda and son Akshay, deserve special mention for putting up with my love for cricket. Akshay, the force behind my work, can actually be termed a 'co-author'. His inputs have been immensely valuable.

Can't forget the help from Prof. Mona Sinha, Rohit Lal and Tanaya, my charming neighbours for 25 years.

I draw strength from my lovely niece, Shruti Mukundan, her parents, PG Mukundan and Kumud; my brother Ajay, who rarely errs in his cricket predictions; three amazing students, Charudatt Prabhu, Niharika Raina and Priya Nagi, for their faith in me that keeps me going.

Thanks to Mona Parthsarthi, Neeru Bhatia, Rahul Rawat, Avishek Roy, Abhishek Roy, Amlan Chakraborty and Udita Dutta for all their good wishes. Chetan Narula, the globetrotting cricket journalist, and GS Vivek have always been very kind.

My colleagues, Kamesh Srinivasan, Rakesh Rao, YB Sarangi, Uthra Ganesan and Abhishek Mukherjee for coping with me.

Finally, grateful to Arnab Karmakar, the young editor with an inbuilt smile, for giving shape to the manuscript.

Vijay Lokapally

I have been a fan of Vijay Lokapally for many years. Therefore, I am truly grateful and honoured for the offer to work with him on this book about the Indian squad headed to England and Wales for the ICC World Cup 2019. Also, thanks to Bloomsbury India for making this dream come true for me.

Over the years, I have been lucky to have worked with the father of Indian comics, the late Anant Pai, ace illustrator, late Pradeep Sathe and renowned sportswriters like Ayaz Memon, late Pradeep Vijayakar, H Natarajan, Clayton Murzello and others. All of them have been very kind to me and have been a constant source of inspiration for my work.

A word of thanks to Rohini Nair and her *Firstpost* team, and Luis Fernandes and Meera Nair of *Dimdima* for keeping me busy with my sports columns.

Finally, thanks to my wife Rina and daughter Natasha, who keep me grounded; my late parents, who would have taken pride in showing off this book to friends and family.

Austin Coutinho

About the Author

Vijay Lokapally has been covering sports for *The Hindu* and *Sportstar* since 1986. Cricket has been close to his heart and considers himself fortunate to have written on a game he has loved so much.

Cricket reporting took him to far corners of the world. He is among the few from India who has sent despatches from literally every venue of the cricketing world.

Lokapally has the distinction of covering his first World Cup in 1987 and later reporting on the editions in 1996, 1999, 2003 and 2011. He considers the 1999 and 2003 travels to England and South Africa for the World Cup the high points of his cricket reportage.

The 1983 World Cup was the trigger point for Lokapally to take to sports journalism and he is proud to count some of the big names of Indian cricket among his friends. He lives in Delhi with wife Sunanda and son Akshay.

About the Illustrator

Austin Coutinho is a caricaturist and sportswriter. A former fast bowler and Mumbai's Ranji probable in the 1980s, he retired from Rashtriya Chemicals & Fertilizers Ltd as the Senior Manager, CRM, in December 2014. A graduate in science and laws, he possesses post-graduate qualifications in journalism, marketing and public relations.

Author of several books, Coutinho has contributed cartoons and sports features to some of the top publications and websites in India. He now writes a weekly column for *Firstpost* and a monthly column for children's magazine, *Dimdima*.

Besides earning renown as a former cricket and football coach, he was at the helm of Mumbai football for a while and was also a member of the state's sports committee.

He lives in Mumbai with wife Rina and daughter Natasha, who is an entertainment writer with *The Times of India*.